The Complete
UNOFFICIALL
Guide to
The Sopranos
Seasons III and IV

By: Kristina Benson

The Complete Unofficial Guide to the Sopranos: Seasons III and IV

ISBN: 978-1-60332-046-7

Edited By: Brooke Winger

Copyright© 2008 Equity Press. No part of this publication may be reproduced, stored in a retrieval system, or transmitted in any form or by any means (electronic, mechanical, photocopying, recording or otherwise) without either the prior written permission of the publisher or a license permitting restricted copying in the United States or abroad.

The scanning, uploading and distribution of this book via the internet or via any other means without the permission of the publisher is illegal and punishable by law. Please purchase only authorized electronic editions, and do not participate in or encourage piracy of copyrighted materials.

Equity Press is not affiliated with HBO, Home Box Office, HBO subsidiaries, A&E, its creator David Chase, any HBO writers or directors.

Trademarks: All trademarks are the property of their respective owners. Equity Press is not associated with any product or vender mentioned in this book.

Printed in the United States of America

Table of Contents

Sopranos Season Three 9

"Mr. Ruggiero's Neighborhood" 11
    Guest Starring 11
    Synopsis 12
    Trivia 13

"Proshai Livushka" 15
    Guest Starring 15
    Synopsis 16
    Hits 18
    First Appearances 18
    Trivia 18

"Fortunate Son" 21
    Guest Starring 21
    Synopsis 22
    First Appearances 24
    Trivia 24

"Employee of the Month" 27
    Guest Starring 27
    Synopsis 28
    First Appearances 30
    Trivia 30

"Another Toothpick" 30
    Guest Starring 31
    Synopsis 31
    Hits 34
    Trivia 35

"University" 37
    Guest Starring 37
    Synopsis 38
    Hits 40
    Themes and Symbolism 40
    Trivia 41

"Second Opinion" 43
    Guest Starring 43
    Synopsis 43
    Trivia 45

"He is Risen" 47
    Guest Starring 47
    Synopsis 48
    First Appearances 49
    Hits 50
    Trivia 50

"The Telltale Moozadell 51
    Guest starring 51
    Synopsis 52
    Trivia 54

"To Save us all from Satan's Power" 55
    Guest Starring 55
    Synopsis 55
    Trivia 58

"Pine Barrens" 59
    Guest Starring 59
    Synopsis 59
    Trivia 62

"Amour Fou" 63
   Guest Starring 63
   Synopsis 64
   Hits 66
   Trivia 67

"Army of One' 69
   Guest Starring 69
   Synopsis 70
   Hits 73
   Trivia 73

Sopranos Season Four 75

"For All Debts Public and Private" 77
   Guest Starring 77
   Synopsis 78
   First Appearances 82
   Hits 83
   Trivia 83

"No Show" 85
   Guest Starring 85
   Synopsis 86
   Trivia 89

"Christopher" 91
   Guest Starring 91
   Synopsis 92

"The Weight" 95
   Guest Starring 95
   Synopsis 96
   Trivia 98

"Pie-O-My" 99
    Guest Starring 99
    Synopsis.. 100
    Trivia 101

"Everybody Hurts" 103
    Guest Starring 103
    Synopsis.. 103
    Trivia 106

"Watching Too Much Television" 109
    Guest Starring 109
    Synopsis.. 110

"Mergers and Acquisitions" 113
    Guest Starring 113
    Synopsis.. 113
    First Appearances 116
    Hits 116
    Trivia 116

"Whoever did this" 117
    Guest Starring 117
    Synopsis.. 117
    Hits 119
    Trivia 119

"The Strong, Silent Type" 121
    Guest Starring 121
    Synopsis.. 122
    Trivia 123

"Calling all Cars" 125
   Guest Starring 125
   Synopsis 126
   First Appearances 130
   Trivia 130

"Eloise" 133
   Guest Starring 133
   Synopsis 134
   Hits 140
   Trivia 140

"Whitecaps" 141
   Guest Starring 141
   Synopsis 142
   Hits 148
   Trivia 148
   Index 150

The Sopranos: Season Three

"Mr. Ruggiero's Neighborhood"

"Mr. Ruggerio's Neighborhood" is the 27th episode of the HBO original series, The Sopranos. It was the first episode for the show's third season. The episode was written by David Chase and was directed by Allen Coulter. It originally aired on Sunday March 4, 2001.

Guest Starring

- Jerry Adler as Hesh Rabkin
- Saundra Santiago as Jeannie Cusamano
- Frank Pellegrino as Bureau Chief Frank Cubitoso
- Louis Lombardi as Agent Skip Lipari
- Matt Servitto as Agent Harris
- Frank Pando as Agent Grasso
- Michele DeCesare as Hunter Scangarelo
- Dan Grimaldi as Patsy Parisi
- Robert Funaro as Eugene Pontecorvo
- John Fiore as Gigi Cestone

Synopsis

After Pussy turns up missing, Agent Lipari remembers that Tony talks business in his basement. If the FBI were to obtain a search warrant, and could gain entry to that basement, they would be able to maintain a high level of surveillance on the Soprano home and business. Agent Cubitoso and Harris go to obtain the court order but are warned by the judge not to linger there for too long. The FBI find a one hour and forty-five minute period each Tuesday when nobody is home. That Tuesday, when the housekeeper goes to English lessons and a picnic with her husband, the FBI break and enter into the Soprano home. In the basement, they find a lamp which could easily hide a microphone. They decide to come back the following Tuesday to plant the device. However, their plan is foiled when water heater explodes and the basement is flooded. The Sopranos are then forced to gather old relics and boxes before they are destroyed by the water. The following week, after the water heater is fixed and the basement is put back in order, the FBI plants the new lamp and quickly leave before the maid arrives back from lunch.

Meanwhile, Meadow is adjusting to life at Columbia University where she meets her very energetic but homesick roommate, Caitlin. AJ is continuing to place little value on his education, cutting classes to smoke cigarettes with friends. Carmela begins taking tennis lessons with Adriana as a distraction.

Tony is still running the DiMeo crime family and is concerned about a possible garbage war involving Barone Sanitation. He then gathers with his friends at Satriale's where he finds Patsy Parisi mourning over his deceased twin brother. Tony acts as if he does not know what actually happened but Patsy knows Tony had something to do with it. The following day while the FBI watches, Patsy aims a gun at Tony from the pool patio. He then puts the gun down and pees in the pool instead.

Trivia

- Mr. Ruggerio is the neighborhood plumber in Tony's area.

- Like Tony in this episode, real-life Mafioso Angelo Ruggiero had his house bugged by the FBI, yielding crucial evidence that lead to the indictment of John Gotti.

- The title is also a reference to the children's television show, Mister Rogers' Neighborhood.

- Although this episode aired first, "Proshai, Livushka" was the first to be shot.

- The episode was part one of a two-hour season premiere when it originally aired in 2001.

- Joe Pantoliano (Ralph Cifaretto), Federico Casteluccio

(Furio Giunta), Steve R. Schirripa (Bobby "Bacala" Baccalieri) and Robert Funaro (Eugene Pontecorvo) are now billed in the opening credits.

"Proshai Livushka"

"Proshai, Livushka" is the 28th episode of the HBO original series, The Sopranos. It was the second episode for the show's third season. The episode was written by David Chase and was directed by Tim Van Patten. It originally aired on Sunday March 4, 2001.

Guest Starring

- Jason Cerbone as Jackie Aprile, Jr.
- Vincent Pastore as Big Pussy Bonpensiero
- Peter Riegert as Ronald Zellman
- Jerry Adler as Hesh Rabkin
- Joseph R. Gannascoli as Vito Spatafore
- Vincent Curatola as Johnny Sack
- Sharon Angela as Rosalie Aprile
- Alla Kliuoka as Svetlana
- Maureen Van Zandt as Gabriella Dante
- Dan Grimaldi as Patsy Parisi
- Robert Funaro as Eugene Pontecorvo
- John Fiore as Gigi Cestone
- Nicole Burdette as Barbara Soprano Giglione
- Ed Vassalo as Tom Giglione
- Mary Shepherd as Mary De Angelis
- Tom Aldredge as Hugh De Angelis

- Patrick Tully as Noah Tannenbaum

Synopsis

Tony succumbs to an anxiety attack and collapses on the floor. When Carmela arrives home, she helps him up and asks what happened. The scene rewinds to Tony greeting Meadow and her new boyfriend. Meadow's boyfriend, Noah Tannenbaum comes out of the bathroom and happily shakes Tony's hand. When Meadow goes upstairs, Tony asks where he is from, what his background it, and says he is a Jewish African-American. Tony, then, instructs Noah to break up with his daughter when they get back to school, and to stay away from her, and then Noah storms out of the house. Meadow, when she comes downstairs and realizes her boyfriend is gone, refuses talk to Tony.

Tony then visits his mother and warns her not to talk to the FBI. Livia becomes uneasy, and fidgety. Svetlana, Livia's nurse, then brings out baby books and asks Livia write some family history. Tony continues to be upset and Livia then says "it is none of anybody's business". Tony then dismissively tells her to do what she wants, then, regarding his upcoming trial and to leave him alone. Later, Tony is gardening in the yard, Carmela gets a call that Livia has passed.

As people begin to gather at the Soprano residence, Barbara informs him that Janice will not be in attendance, and in front of his guests, Tony says Janice is "a motherfucking bitch". He then calls her at home in Seattle and demands she be on the next plane to New Jersey. Janice reminds Tony she has a good reason not to be in the State of New Jersey since she shot and killed Richie months prior after he punched her in the mouth. Tony tells her "the case is colder than her tit" and to come anyway. The next morning, Janice arrives and rapidly becomes the center of attention.

At the funeral home, Tony and Barbara arrange the service and Janice objects, angling for a fancy ceremony. Tony tells her that he does not want any "California bullshit" and just a simple, pious service with a party afterward. Everyone prepares for the wake the following evening, including Silvio, who is angry because he is missing football in order to pay respects, and Ray Curto, who is wearing a wire. Uncle Junior tries to reconcile with Carmela with mixed results. The next day at the cemetery, Livia is buried and Meadow shys away from Tony. Afterwards, Janice informs Svetlana she will be living at Livia's home and would like the records she took back by the weekend.

Janice then thinks it's a good idea if everyone gives a little speech about Livia. Livia is eulogized by Hesh, Christopher, and her friend, after which Carmela interrupts claiming this is a "crock of shit". She then proceeds to say how Livia did not want a funeral because she thought no one would come, and alludes to the ways in which Livia challenged and denigrated whoever was around her. This seems to satisfy everyone there other than Janice, and Carmela's mother, who are infuriated.

Later, as Tony watches the final moments of the film The Public

Enemy he begins to cry.

Hits

- Livia Soprano: dies of massive stroke in her sleep

First Appearances

- Ralph Cifaretto: soldier in the Aprile crew which is headed at this time by Gigi Cestone.

Trivia

- Russian translation for "Good Bye, Little Livia", which Svetlana says as she, Carmela and Tony toast Livia.

- Although this episode aired second, it was the first to be shot.

- Because Nancy Marchand passed, David Chase decided that the character of Livia should die as well and resurrected her using CGI with previous sound clips and scenes featuring Marchand. The cost was approximately $250,000.

- This is the final episode where Nancy Marchand is billed in the opening credits.

- David Chase had planned a major story line for the third season concerning Tony's efforts to patch things up with his mother to prevent her from testifying against him at his RICO trial. However, the death of the actress that plays Livia caused Chase to revise a large portion of the season.

- The episode was part two of a two-hour season premiere when it originally aired in 2001.

- Vincent Pastore makes a cameo in this episode when Tony opens a closet door and Pussy is seen in the mirror.

"Fortunate Son"

"Fortunate Son" is the 29th episode of the HBO original series, The Sopranos. It was the 3rd episode for the show's third season. The episode was written by Todd A. Kessler and was directed by Henry J. Bronchtein. It originally aired on Sunday March 11, 2001.

Guest Starring

- Jason Cerbone as Jackie Aprile, Jr.
- Vince Curatola as Johnny Sack
- Joseph Siravo as Johnny Boy Soprano
- George Loros as Raymond Curto
- Tony Darrow as Larry Boy Barese
- Richard Maldone as Ally Boy Barese
- Sharon Angela as Rosalie Aprile
- Oksana Lada as Irina Peltsin
- Alla Kliouka Schaffer as Svetlana Kirilenko
- Robert Funaro as Eugene Pontecorvo
- John Fiore as Gigi Cestone

Synopsis

Paulie Walnuts pages Christopher, and Christopher is given instructions to meet at a shopping center parking lot in an hour and to "look sharp". After shaving and dressing and sharing a moment with Adriana, he drives to Modell's, hoping that this is his ceremony for being made. Silvio then drives up along with Paulie and they all get into the car. They are then driven to a basement of a made man where Tony congratulates Christopher and Eugene, who is also being made. Tony continues his speech to say that if they have any doubts to speak up now since "once [they] enter this family, there's no getting out". He reminds them that mob life comes before anything else, even blood family, and if a soldier's health problems prevent him from earning, he can count on his crew for assistance. Tony then asks for their hands and draws blood by pricking them with a needle. He gives them both a picture of St. Peter which they then light on fire in their hands. Tony then asks them to repeat the phrase "May I burn in hell if I betray my friends". Christopher nervously eyes a raven which has landed on the open window, fearing it to be a bad omen.

After the ceremony, Tony throws a lavish celebration at Nuovo Vesuvio with food and strippers from the Bing. Paulie congratulates Christopher for being made and enumerates what his new responsibilities will be. Seeing as Christopher is now officially in the family, Paulie's sportsbook is now his and he will have to give Paulie a minimum amount of money each week or he will begin getting points added on. Christopher tells Paulie that he loves him and looks forward to working with him.

However, Christopher later finds out that the sportsbook is not bringing in as much money as anticipated, but he still gives the small sum of money he has to Paulie. Paulie, in turn, Paulie warns Christopher to give him the money by the end of the week with another $2,000.00. Christopher then receives an tip from the late Jackie Aprile's son, Jackie Jr. that he plans to rob a benefit concert at Rutgers University. Jackie acts as driver and Christopher robs the ticket booth at gunpoint, giving the money to Paulie. .

Tony asks Dr. Melfi about his progress, and what direction they are going in since he is still suffers from anxiety attacks out. Dr. Melfi suggests a behavior therapist but Tony feels that he is not ready. Melfi then becomes angered when Tony answers his phone, claiming that it is "his busy season" and he has to take it. He then manages to recall the details of his first panic attack. At 12 years old, Tony witnesses his father cut off the pinky of Mr. Satriale, who owned the pork store during the 1960s. At dinner that evening, Johnny Boy—Tony's father-- tells Tony that Mr. Satriale is a degenerate gambler that owed money and that was his punishment. Tony then feels better but when he watches his mother get excited when she cuts the roast, Tony passes out. Melfi thinks that this is a break through since several of his panic attacks have to do with the presence of meat. Tony claims it is a coincidence but that he does find it weird that Livia got "turned on by free meat".

Meanwhile, Anthony Jr. has joined the school football team. When AJ recovers a fumble at a game, Tony becomes extremely happy and enthusiastic, and voices his suggestion that AJ become more devoted to the sport, but AJ claims he'd rather pass time playing Nintendo. Meadow continues not to talk to Tony, and Carmela tries to convince Meadow she does not know anything about their quarrel but Meadow says that everyone knows, and the situation would never have happened if Noah was white. While touring the Columbia University campus, AJ becomes dizzy and nervous as he gets anxious about college. Later, at football practice, after being promoted to defensive captain, AJ passes out on the field.

First Appearances

- Carmine Lupertazzi: Boss of the Lupertazzi Crime family, one of five New York mob organizations.

Trivia

- The title refers the song "Fortunate Son" by Creedence Clearwater Revival, a song about spoiled and privileged American youth.

- In this and future episodes Christopher references the raven he sees during his making ceremony as a bad omen.

- When Adriana learns that Christopher is about to be made, she becomes worried that it might be a pretext for a hit. When Christopher arrives, Silvio tells Tony that Chris was nervous during the entire ride over. In both cases, reference is made to "watching too many movies". This is a reference to Goodfellas, where Tommy is lured to his death in a cornfield under the pretext of being made.

"Employee of the Month"

"Employee of the Month" is the 30th episode of the HBO original series, The Sopranos. It was the 4th episode for the show's third season. The episode was written by Robin Green & Mitchell Burgess and was directed by John Patterson. It originally aired on Sunday March 18, 2001.

Guest Starring

- Jason Cerbone as Jackie Aprile, Jr.
- Vince Curatola as Johnny Sack
- Peter Bogdanovich as Dr. Elliott Kupferburg
- Sharon Angela as Rosalie Aprile
- Oksana Lada as Irina Peltsin
- Peter Riegert as Ronald Zellman
- Denise Borino as Ginny Sacrimoni
- Richard Romanus as Richard La Penna
- Will McCormack as Jason La Penna
- Mario Polit as Jesus Rossi
- Robert Funaro as Eugene Pontecorvo
- John Fiore as Gigi Cestone

Synopsis

In Tony's next session, Dr. Melfi tells him that he is ready to see a behavioral therapist, thinking that Tony will take this as a good thing since it comes in the wake of a breakthrough. Tony, however, is hurt and thinks that she is trying to get rid of him. She quickly changes the subject, making small talk with Tony about his family, and then Dr. Melfi suggests that he bring Carmela into the therapy sessions. Tony feels uncomfortable about the idea, fearing the consequences, but agrees to ask Carmela anyway.

Meanwhile, Johnny Sack and his wife move to New Jersey without sharing the plans of this move with anyone beforehand. They are surprised to receive a visit from Tony, who is upset because Johnny had not previously mentioned anything about the move. Johnny explains that Ginny wants to be closer to her sisters and that they already had a condo in Point Pleasant, New Jersey, and he assures Tony that he will not get invovled in or interfere with Soprano business. He then invites Tony and some of his associates to a housewarming party.

Later in the evening, as Dr. Melfi leaves the office, she is attacked in the parking structure by a young man named Jesus Rossi, who pushes her into a stairwell. He brutally rapes her and leaves her crying for help. She is taken to the emergency room for a rape kit, her leg and face badly bruised. Her son, Jason, wants revenge, but Richard (Melfi's ex-husband) tells Jason to let the police handle it. The following day, they learn that Rossi was released from police custody on a technicality. Dr. Melfi, knowing that he is out on the streets, is nervous and afraid, her fear compromising her ability to complete even mundane tasks. While buying a sandwich, she notices a plaque indicating that Jesus Rossi is the name of the "Employee of the Month." Upset, drops her soda and runs out of the building.

That night, she dreams about buying a soda at a vending machine and getting her hand trapped in the machine. While trapped, she dreams of a large Rotweiler that attacks and kills her rapist.Later, she describes the dream to her therapist, Dr. Elliott Kupferberg, and thinks that the large dog protecting her symbolized Tony Soprano, the one man who could take revenge on her behalf

Ralphie Cifaretto begins to show a fatherly interest in Jackie Jr., the son of his girlfriend, Rosalie Aprile. During dinner at Nuovo Vesuvio, Ralph asks Jackie if he has any interest in Meadow Soprano. Shortly thereafter, Ralph takes him to help collect money from a client who refuses to pay up, goading the man into a fight. The client swings a bat at Jackie but they still manage to take the man's wallet. Hearing of this, Tony warns Ralph to keep Jackie away from the family, as he had promised Jackie Sr. before he died.

The Russian mob comes to visit Janice after she still has refused to give up Svetlana's leg. They Russians beat her badly and force her to get the leg, which is in a locker in a bowling alley. Tony visits Janice at the hospital and she tells him that she has "found God" and has forgiven Svetlana for what happened.

When Dr. Melfi becomes upset, and starts to cry during Tony's next therapy session, he asks her what is wrong, and if she wants to tell him anything. After a long and tense pause, Melfi declines.

First Appearances

- Ginny Sacrimoni: The wife of Johnny Sack

Trivia

- The episode's writers, Robin Green & Mitchell Burgess, won an Emmy award in 2001 for Best Writing in a Drama Series.

- According to creator David Chase, Melfi's rape case is likely to remain unsolved.

- Ralph makes a reference to his son Justin, whom viewers meet in "Whoever Did This".

- Denise Borino (Ginny Sack) had never acted professionally before.

"Another Toothpick"

"Another Toothpick" is the 31st episode of the HBO original series, The Sopranos. It was the 5th episode for the show's third season. The episode was written by Terence Winter and was directed by Jack Bender. It originally aired on Sunday March 25, 2001.

Guest Starring

- # Jackie Aprile, Jr.
- # Peter Riegert as Ronald Zellman
- # Vince Curatola as Johnny Sack
- # Charles S. Dutton as Officer Leon Wilmore
- # Joseph R. Gannascoli as Vito Spatafore
- # Paul Schulze as Father Phil Intintola
- # Kathrine Narducci as Charmaine Bucco
- # Suzanne Shepherd as Mary De Angelis
- # Tom Aldredge as Hugh De Angelis
- # Matt Servitto as Agent Harris
- # Frank Pellegrino as Bureau Chief Frank Cubitoso
- # Brian Tarantina as Mustang Sally
- # Burt Young as Bobby Bacala, Sr.
- # Robert Funaro as Eugene Pontecorvo
- # John Fiore as Gigi Cestone

Synopsis

When Tony brings Carmela to his next session with Dr. Melfi, Tony remains quiet while Carmela asks Melfi questions. Melfi then asks if Tony has been talking to Carmela about any of the origins of his "root causes". Carmela at first can't remember and then Tony reminds about the finger incident from Satriale's that he witnessed as a child. Carmela, first asking Melfi why Tony still passes out, then yells "maybe it's because you stick your dick into anything that has a pulse, can that be considered that a root cause". Dr. Melfi quietly observes "I'm sensing tension", prompting Tony to remark that she "must been at the top of [her] fucking class".

After the session is over, Carmela cries on the ride home, and Tony, also tense, exceeds the speed limit and is pulled over, and given a ticket. Tony then gets in calls his government contact Assemblyman Ronald Zellman, who says he will look into the situation. Days after, he runs into the cop at a gardening store, and Leon (the cop) tells him that thanks to Tony, he was fired. Tony later calls Zellman, and Zellman says that Officer Willmore was let go because he had issues within the force. Still, Tony feels guilty and asks if the cop can have his job back, but later he has a change of heart and tells Zellman to forget it. .

Later, after attending a funeral for Carmela's uncle, Tony meets up with Bobby Bacala and his father Bobby, Sr, who is suffering from lung cancer and has impaired breathing as a result.

When a thug, Mustang Sally, clubs Vito Spatafore's cousin Bryan and puts him in the hospital, Bobby Sr. agrees to do the hit since he is his godfather. His son, however, fears that his father's health is too poor and asks Junior to convince Tony to ask someone else to do it. Bobby Sr, meanwhile, impatient, proceeds to visit Mustang Sally's house in Staten Island. After Sally turns to get him a glass of water, Bobby shoots him in the ear. They then fight and Bobby shoots Sally and his friend Carlos. As he leaves, he smokes Sally's cigs int he car. After he drops his inhaler, he cannot breathe and loses control of the car, crashing into a pole.

Junior then tells Tony at Dr. Schreck's office that he has cancer. He asks Tony not to tell anyone, but Tony tells Janice and they both meet at Livia's for a drink and discuss Janice's new ferver for faith.

During an argument in the Soprano household between Tony and Meadow about Tony's unapologetic ferver for racism, Meadow takes the lamp that holds the bug that the FBI planted. She says she wants it for her dorm room cause the halogen lights are making her sick.

Meanwhile, Adriana tells Artie that she is quitting her job at Nuovo Vesuvia because as a made guy, Christopher is making more money. Artie doesn't take it well, insulting Christopher and inciting a fight which Tony breaks up. Artie tells Tony that he is in love with Adriana, but Tony tells him to sober up, and never say that again. He tells Artie he has a proposal for him, which they talk about the next day. Tony proposes that he and Artie go into business together selling Italian food and products.

Charmaine, however, is not in love with the idea of doing business with a known mobster, and after expressing her usual scorn for Tony, takes it further and threatens divorce. He doesn't take her threat very seriously, which angers her even more, and she tells him that it's over. Artie later has an awkward dinner with Adriana in the auspices of a "good-bye meal", taking her hand repeatedly and trying to convince her that she is not ready to be married.

Hits

- Febby Viola: died of cancer; Carmela's uncle
- Mustang Sally: shot on orders by Tony Soprano and Gigi Cestone
- Carlos: Mustang: Sally's friend who was shot for being a witness to his murder
- Bobby Bacala, Sr.: cause unknown; either from cancer or a collision caused when he dropped his inhaler.

Trivia

- During Junior's tirade, when he smashes the picture frame, he can briefly be seen without his glasses, then a second later they are back on.

- Janice claims that Livia often said this when a person was about to die of cancer because of the emaciated appearance that comes with metastatic illness.

"University"

"University" is the 32nd episode of the HBO original series, The Sopranos. It was the 6th episode for the show's third season. The episode's teleplay was written by Terence Winter and Salvatore J. Stabile with a story idea by David Chase & Terence Winter & Todd A. Kessler and Robin Green & Mitchell Burgess and was directed by Allen Coulter. It originally aired on Sunday April 1, 2001.

Guest Starring

- Jason Cerbone as Jackie Aprile, Jr.
- Ariel Kiley as Tracee
- Sharon Angela as Rosalie Aprile
- Suzanne Shepherd as Mary De Angelis
- Tom Aldredge as Hugh De Angelis
- John Fiore as Gigi Cestone

Synopsis

One afternoon at the Bada Bing, a dancer named Tracee tries to give Tony homemade bread to show her thanks for Tony's help when she needed a good doctor for her son. Tony is very thankful for the bread but says he can't accept it because the dancers are not supposed to be friends with their clients. Tracee takes it well, apologizing for the misstep.

Meanwhile at Columbia University, Meadow has continued to see her boyfriend Noah despite her father's objections. As she and Noah start to kiss, Meadow's roommate Caitlin walks in and interrupts their kiss, asking if she could keep them company since she is freaked out by a horror film she saw with friends.. Noah and Meadow decide to cheer Caitlin up by taking her out for her birthday. The outing, however, takes a turn for the worse when Caitlin is upset by the off-kilter appearance of a bag lady, sending Caitlin to sob back at the dorm room.

Meadow, tired of the drama inspired by Caitlin's home sickneess, decides to go to the Soprano home. When she does so, she then tells her mother that she is growing closer and closer to Noah and that she is in love. Carmela tells her that she can do as she please but not to tell her father. Later, Meadow meets Noah's father for dinner one evening and they ask Meadow about her parents, and what they do. The following day, Noah breaks it off with Meadow.

Tracee continues to woo Tony, following him to his car one afternoon to confide in him that she is pregnant with Ralphie's baby. She doesnt know whether to keep the baby, or abort it. Tony warns her that because she has had domestic abuse before with her other son, and that the child is Ralphie's "[she] would be doing his kid's generations a huge favor". He keeps the news to himself and doesn't tell Ralphie.

Ralphie, however, doesn't act as though he's particularly concerned about the situation. As he becomes riveted by the movie Gladiator, he begins to shout out quotes from the film and plays around roughly with Georgie at the V.I.P. lounge, getting carried away and swinging a chain at Georgie. Tony, meanwhile, has been trying to enjoy a blowjob but is forced to discontinue receiving it when Ralphie temporarily blinds Georgie with a metal chain. He then sends Ralphie to escort Georgie to the hospital. A few days later, Tracee has not showed up for work. Silvio then goes to her home where she is cooking for Ralphie and watching television. He forces her to get dressed and slaps her as she is entering his car. Ralphie finds the entire scene hilarious.

The following night, Ralphie sees Tracee at the V.I.P. lounge and she insults him vociferously and venomously in front of everyone. Ralphie then follows her out to the deserted Bada Bing parking lot and after chit chat about baby names, he calls her a whore. She manages to land one punch before Ralphie beats her to death. It is not long before her body is found, and Tony becomes very upset, punching Ralphie and yelling that he disrepected the Bing.

Tony continues to takes Tracee's death very badly and becomes very emotional during a therapy session with Carmela and Dr. Melfi. He lies, however, and says that a young associate from Barone Sanitation died. Days later, the Bada Bing strippers wonder where Tracee went and conclude that she left with Ralphie and never came back.

Hits

- Tracee: Bada Bing stripper beat to death by Ralphie in the parking lot

Themes and Symbolism

- Throughout the episode, scenes between Ralphie and Tracee are as bookends to scenes between Meadow and Noah. The comparison is striking in that we see that women in a classy, educational setting aren't treated much differently than women in a strip club.

Trivia

- The song during the beginning and ending credits is "Living on a Thin Line" by The Kinks. According to Terence Winter, it is the series' most asked about song.

- According to actress Ariel Kiley who plays Tracee "A lot of subscribers canceled their HBO service because of those episodes. Nothing against HBO, but I was proud of that."

"Second Opinion"

"Second Opinion" is the 33rd episode of the HBO original series, The Sopranos. It was the 7th episode for the show's third season. The episode was written by Lawrence Konner and was directed by Tim Van Patten. It originally aired on Sunday April 8, 2001

Guest Starring

- Sam McMurray as Dr. John Kennedy
- Sully Boyar as Dr. Krakower
- Dan Grimaldi as Patsy Parisi
- Toni Kalem as Angie Bonpensiero
- Suzanne Shepherd as Mary De Angelis
- Tom Aldredge as Hugh De Angelis

Synopsis

Uncle Junior is put under anesthesia for his surgery to remove the malignant tumors in his digestive system. After he is put under, he experiences a dream sequence in which the FBI offers to cure his cancer if he will work for them. A newspaper then appears on screen featuring the following headline: SOPRANO WINS FREEDOM, INDICTS NEPHEW.

While Junior is going through his surgery, Dr. Kennedy tells the friends and family that have come to his side that he will be ok, and they have managed to remove the tumor. But after a following visit to the doctor's office, Dr. Kennedy informs Junior and Bobby Bacala that they have found more malignant cells and would once again like to perform surgery. Uncle Junior begins to concede but Tony urges him to get a second opinion. Tony and Uncle Junior then consult with another doctor in New York City who recommends chemotherapy. Junior does so but still awaits hearing from Dr. Kennedy, who is not returning any of his calls. The doc is then paid a visit on the golf course and when Tony approaches him to strongly advise that he start taking Junior's calls, and the sooner the better.

Carmela, meanwhile, visits Dr. Melfi without Tony and begins to break down crying as she confides that she knows little about Tony's job and lifestyle, and that she is depressed. Melfi recommends that she see a colleague in Livingston, Dr. Krakower, if she would like to see a therapist on a regular basis. Carmela reluctantly calls Dr. Krakower, and during the session, she discusses her husband's profession . The therapist recommends that she file for dicorce, and refuses to accept any payment for the session but advises her to leave while she still can.

Christopher is angered when Paulie asks him if he is wearing a wire. Christopher denies as such and becomes enraged as he is forced to take his clothes off—even his undergarments. Then at 2 am, Paulie and Patsy pay an unexpected visit to his apartment under the guise of looking for anyhting suspicious. Christopher becomes extremely angered when Paulie takes all of Adriana's new shoes for his own mistress and sniffs Adriana's panties. Christopher tells Tony this the following day but is soon chastised by Paulie who warns him never to go over his head again about an argument. They agree to settle the argument after Christopher leaves a motel room with another woman.

Meanwhile Carmela spots Angie Bonpensiero in Pathmark and decides to invite her to dinner. Angie politely rejects the offer saying that her dog is very sick and that she can't afford her veterinarian bills now that Pussy has disappeared. Tony, then, pays Angie a visit. Tony spots Angie's new Cadillac in the driveway and breaks the window to beep the horn, and when the dog comes trotting out with her, it's clear that he is in good health. Tony then tells her that if she needs money to not ask Carmela but to come directly to him.

Trivia

- Mike Nichols was originally cast to play the role of Dr. Krakower, and original broadcast, Nichols was credited instead of Boyar. However during re-airings and on the DVD, Sully Boyar is correctly credited.

- The episode features the toy Big Mouth Billy Bass, a popular singing robotic fish from the late 1990's

"He is Risen"

"He Is Risen" is the 34th episode of the HBO original series, The Sopranos. It was the 8th episode for the show's third season. The episode was written by Robin Green & Mitchell Burgess and Todd A. Kessler and was directed by Allen Coulter. It originally aired on Sunday April 15, 2001.

Guest Starring

- Jason Cerbone as Jackie Aprile, Jr.
- Jerry Adler as Hesh Rabkin
- Tom Alderidge as Hugh De Angelis
- Annabella Sciorra as Gloria Trillo
- Suzanne Shepherd as Mary De Angelis
- Sharon Angela as Rosalie Aprile
- Joseph R. Gannascoli as Vito Spatafore
- Robert Funaro as Eugene Pontecorvo
- John Fiore as Gigi Cestone
- Turk Pipkin as Aaron Arkaway

Synopsis

As Tony goes Dr. Melfi's office for his regular appointment it becomes clear that two patients were accidentally booked in the same time slot. The other patient is an attractive, Italian woman named Gloria Trillo who works for Globe Motors. Tony, of course, is instantly attracted to her and also intrigued as to why she is there. Melfi reminds Tony that she cannot discuss her patients.

As Thanksgiving draws near, Tony is still angered, feeling resentment towards Ralphie for beating Tracee to death, maintaining his position that Ralphie "insulted the Bing". Ralphie, however, disagrees with this assessment, and refuses to greet Tony, and also refuses to have a drink with him. Tony becomes extremely irritated and remembering that Ralphie and Ro are set to join them for the Thanksgiving dinner, forces Carmela to lie to Ro, saying there will not be a Thanksgiving this year due to Carmela's father's sickness.

Ro believes the fib. She and Carmela have both noticed that Meadow and Jackie are starting a relationship, and while Ro approves, Carmela is wary. After Thanksgiving dinner, Jackie picks up Meadow under the auspices of taking her to a movie. They end up making out in a parked car near Hunter Scangerello's. Meadow warns Jackie that their relationship is not likely to go anywhere. Days later, Meadow gets drunk and takes Jackie's car keys. Jackie runs after her to prevent her from driving however Meadow is already in the car. She then drives off an on-ramp and totals the car.

Johnny Sack, meanwhile, advises Ralphie to give Tony a genuine apology and Ralphie reluctantly agrees. Johnny Sack informs Tony ahead of time, and wants him to give something to Ralph as a gesture of goodwill. Johnny suggests elevating Ralph to the rank of Capo but Tony refuses. At Vesuvio, Ralphie approaches Tony while he's eating and is not invited to sit. Tony merely curtly asks what he wishes to see him for. Ralphie gives a humble apology, including an "I'm sorry" for turning down Tony's request for a drink and killing Tracee. Ralphie ends up leaving after apologizing, without being offered anything from Tony, not even a place to sit, which infuriates him and he again approaches Johnny to tell him that he's ready to take out Tony. However events take an unexpected turn when Gigi Cestone, capo of the Aprile crew is found dead on the toilet, and Tony is forced by circumstance to make Ralph captain. Tony tells him at Vesuvio, and Ralphie is ecstatic but also wondering if Tony did this because of Gigi's death. Tony tells him to just be happy with the decision that has been made. Ralphie then asks if he is going to join him for a drink but Tony gets up and leaves.

Tony then visits Globe Motors and asks Gloria if she will accompany him on a test drive. They end up on the Stugots (Tony's boat) and make love, and Gloria cancels her appointment with Dr. Melfi so she can be with him.

First Appearances

- Gloria Trillo: a therapy patient of Dr. Melfi's and a saleswoman at Globe Motors.
- Little Paulie Germani: Paulie Walnuts' nephew and crew member.

Hits

- Gigi Cestone: dies from complications of heart disease

- **Trivia**

- The Song played over the end credits is "The Captain" by Kasey Chambers.

- When Tony confronts Jackie, Jr. at the casino, the song playing under the scene is "Black Hearted Woman" by The Allman Brothers Band.

"The Telltale Moozadell

"The Telltale Moozadell" is the 35th episode of the HBO original series, The Sopranos. It was the 9th episode for the show's third season. The episode was written by Michael Imperioli and was directed by Dan Attias. It originally aired on Sunday April 22, 2001.

Guest starring

- Jason Cerbone as Jackie Aprile, Jr.
- Andrew Davoli as Dino Zerilli
- Louis Crugnali as Carlo Renzi
- Nick Tarabay as Matush
- Jerry Adler as Hesh
- Annabella Sciorra as Gloria Trillo
- Max Casella as Benny Fazio
- Will McCormack as Jason La Penna
- Tom Aldredge as Hugh De Angelis
- Suzanne Shepherd as Mary De Angelis
- Sharon Angela as Rosalie Aprile
- Turk Pipkin as Aaron Arkaway

Synopsis

On Carmela's birthday, Tony gives her a sapphire ring. Anthony Jr gives her The Matrix on DVD, and Meadow gives her mother a gift certificate to a day spa, which she put on her mother's credit card. At Carmela's birthday party, Jackie Jr. arrives just as they are about to sing "Happy Birthday" and afterwards, AJ is invited to a friend's house to spend the night, and Meadow and Jackie go to the movies. Carmela asks Tony why he didn't end up buying the Mercedes he was test-driving, and he says that he just didnt think that the car was for him.

In truth, Tony is continuing his affair withGloria Trillo, who, unbeknownst to him, is seeing Dr. Melfi to come to terms with her suicidal past. On their next date, they go to the Bronx zoo and have sex in the reptile house. On their next outing, Gloria finds his gun, but seems impressed and titillated by it rather than scared or perhaps concerned for her safety. At his therapy session with Melfi, he tells her that he has had a very successful week and gives her a bonus, but Melfi declines it. However when her son Jason calls and is in need of expensive textbooks, she has second thoughts about not taking it.

On the night of Carmela's birthday, AJ and friends break into their high school and swim in the pool. When they are finished swimming, a few people begin to throw objects in the pool including desks, trophies and garbage cans, with the situation soon getting out of hand. Later, when the police arrive, they find a pizza that looks like a special order. They then figure out where the pizza came from, and interrogate the owner of the pizza parlor who points them to AJ. Anthony Jr. is sent home from school due to his involvement in the vandalism. Tony and Carmela ground AJ for 2 months and is tell him to take on the chore of cleaning out the rain gutters as punishment, but are slightly mortified when AJ doesn't even know what a rain gutter is.

Christopher buys Adriana "The Lollipop Club," a dance club in Long Branch, New Jersey which she renames "The Crazy Horse." Christopher feels bad that Adriana is no longer working, but is buoyed because she will be able to run her own business, even though he and Furio own a percentage as "silent partners". In addition to giving Adriana a chance to earn her own money, Chris also sees the club as an opportunity for the mob to run their business in an environment which will be unfettered and in which they'll be kings of the hill. However, at the opening of the club, a drug dealer named Matush is caught dealing drugs in the bathroom and is soon warned to get out and stay out. Jackie Jr., however, is friends with Matush, and asks Christopher to let him deal in the club. Christopher flatly refuses. Not wanting to be embarrassed, Jackie Jr. lies to Matush and tells him that Christopher is ok with Matush making deals outside the club. Matush does so, but Christopher's men beat him for it.

Carmela is still concerned about Meadow's relationship with Jackie Jr. but Tony assures Carmela that Jackie is a good kid who will treat their daughter well. Carmela must hide her true feelings to remain friends with Rosalie Aprile, who is ecstatic about the fact that her son is dating Carmela's daughter. Meadow helps Jackie with an Edgar Allan Poe assignment, and he receives an "A." After Tony has a heart-to-heart with Jackie, telling him he will be keeping an eye on him, he promises Tony that he will work hard and be faithful to Meadow. Tony. But the next morning at breakfast, Carmela tells Tony that Jackie took Meadow to see Aida, and Tony has second thoughts.

Trivia

- The episode's title is a play on Edgar Allan Poe's poem, The Tell-Tale Heart. Moozadell is rough Italian slang for mozzarella cheese, but can also be used as a derogatory name for an Italian man.

- "The Lollipop Club" was once owned by Vincent Pastore (Big Pussy Bonpensiero) in real life.

- AJ's birthday present to Carmella is a copy of The Matrix, which featured Joe Pantoliano, who plays Ralph Cifaretto.

"To Save us all from Satan's Power"

Guest Starring

- Jason Cerbone as Jackie Aprile, Jr.
- Matthew Cerbone as Jackie Aprile, Jr. (flashback sequences)
- Andrew Davoli as Dino Zerilli
- Michael Rispoli as Jackie Aprile
- Vincent Pastore as Sal "Big Pussy" Bonpensiero
- Joe Badulucco as Jimmy Altieri
- George Loros as Raymond Curto
- Robert Funaro as Eugene Pontecorvo
- Dan Grimaldi as Patsy Parisi
- Maureen Van Zandt as Gabriella Dante
- Jerry Adler as Hesh Rabkin
- Vitali Baganov as Valery
- Turk Pipkin as Aaron Arkaway
- John Fiore as Gigi Cestone

Synopsis

Before meeting Paulie Walnuts at Asbury Park, Tony muses over an incident back in Christmas of 1995 where he first realized that Pussy wasn't acting normally. When Tony asks if Paulie feels guilty about the shooting, he claims he does not regret it for a second and would do it again. Silvio, however, has begun to have nightmares regarding Pussy, especially when he and Paulie have to find a replacement to play Santa Claus at the Satriale's Christmas party. They decide to choose Bobby Bacala because he looks the part but Bobby proves a terrible Santa, flatly unwilling and unable to effectively spread Christmas cheer. After a child curses at Bobby, Tony goes over to tell Bobby to be a little more positive and upbeat, with some holiday spirit.. Later Paulie jokingly recommends that next year Bobby "goes to Santa School."

Tony realizes that Pussy was coerced into FBI cooperation on a particular night when he missed a sit down with Uncle Junior. Tony also comes to the conclusion that because Pussy refused to let anyone help him with his costume and arrived already dressed as Santa to last year's party, he must have been wearing a wire.

Meanwhile, Janice announces that she will cook Christmas dinner since Carmela does so much cooking for her. When Janice tells Tony that her wrist is increasingly painful, Tony asks how she injured it in the first place. Janice replies that the pain began right after her encounter with the Russian mobster who arrived to retrieve Svetlana's prosthetic leg. Tony then adds to his list of Christmas gifts: Janice's Russian. As a favor to Tony, the boss of the Russian mob gives Tony the name of Janice's attacker-Igor- and where Tony can find him. The following evening, Tony and Furio get into Igor's taxi, beat him, and leave him behind a nativity scene-inspired mall display. The following day on the news, the reporter suggests that a youth street gang was responsible. Janice sees this on the news and in response, she adds another verse to her Christian rock song praising brotherhood.

At Nuovo Vesuvio, the newly separated Charmaine Bucco has never looked better and begins to receive compliments about her appearance from several mob associates. As Tony, Paulie and Silvio eat dinner, Charmaine jokes that there are FBI agents at the next table, causing Silvio to be offended, and Artie to apologize. .The following day, Charmaine tells Tony that she does not want him and "his boys" there all the time and that he ruined their marriage. Tony becomes angered and he, Silvio and Christopher leave. They decide to go to a new strip club where they see Jackie Jr. getting a lap dance from a stripper. Infuriated to see his daughter's boyfriend getting a lapdance, Tony drags him into the bathroom and beats him savagely.

On Christmas, the Sopranos open their gifts. Jackie arrives and gives Meadow a necklace with the engraving "To M.S. from J.A.: I will always be true". Disgusted, Tony takes Jackie into the kitchen where Jackie tells him that he "flunked out" of Rutgers University. Tony reminds him that his father did not want him to enter mob life, and that despite flunking out of college he should keep his nose clean, but Jackie assures Tony that he still has his priorities straight and still will be good to Meadow. Jackie then leaves to drive his mother to a nursing home to visit his grandmother. Returning to his family, Tony is unnerved when he gets a Big Mouth Billy Bass from Meadow, reminding him of the dream that revealed Pussy's treachery to him.

Trivia

- Tony's deductions about Big Pussy's betrayal timeline are probably wrong; in season two, FBI Agent Skip Lipari reminds Big Pussy that he's been working for them since 1998, not 1995 Tony calculated.

- In the flashback sequences, Jason Cerbone's younger brother, Matthew, portrays Jackie Jr.

- In Silvio's dream, Silvio is standing in front of a clock that gives 2 different times during the same scene.

"Pine Barrens"

"Pine Barrens" is the 37th episode of the HBO original series, The Sopranos. It was the 11th episode for the show's third season. The episode's teleplay was written by Terence Winter and a story idea by Winter & Tim Van Patten and was directed by Steve Buscemi. It originally aired on Sunday May 6, 2001. Many fans have called it the best episode in the show's history.

Guest Starring

- Jason Cerbone as Jackie Aprile, Jr.
- Annabella Sciorra as Gloria Trillo
- Tom Aldredge as Hugh De Angelis
- Suzanne Shepherd as Mary De Angelis
- Oksana Lada as Irina Peltsin
- Vitali Baganov as Valery

Synopsis

After Silvio comes down with a bad case of the flu, Paulie and Christopher make collections on his behalf. One involves an associate of the Russian mob, Valery. While making the collection, Paulie makes fun of the Russian and deliberately destroys his universal remote control, causing Valery to insult Paulie and Christopher, which in turn motivates them to attack him. Paulie chokes Valery with a lamp, and they conclude that he is dead when his breathing stops. They then decide to wrap him in a blanket, put his body in the trunk, and dump it at the Pine Barrens since it is deserted and is close to Atlantic City.

Meanwhile in North Jersey, Tony is with Gloria on his boat when he receives a call from his former cumare Irina, and takes the call in front of Gloria. Jealous, Gloria throws Tony's Christmas gift into the marina and leaves, later making up when she buys him a new gift and they then sleep together. However when Tony is late to a dinner Gloria prepared, she throws the steak at him and sends him out the door.

Meadow also has come down with an illness, and is trying to look to Jackie Jr for comfort. However, when Jackie continues to leave early and fails to make any new dates with Meadow, she follows him and learns he is sleeping with someone else. Meadow then gets out of the car and tearfully breaks up with him, and goes to the hospital shortly after.

In the woods, Christopher and Paulie open the trunk to find that Valery is still alive and has chewed through the carpet tape. They lift him out of the car, present him with a shovel, and demand that he dig his own grave. Not willing to go down that easy, and certainly not willing to dig his own grave if he's going to die anyway, Valery waits till an opportune moment arrives, and smacks them both in the head with the shovel. Christopher and Paulie draw their guns and chase after Valery, but are amazed when he outruns them even after sustaining a shot to the head.

Attempting to follow him, they only manage to kill a deer by mistake. Now lost in the woods, Paulie uses his cellphone to call Tony for help, but he can't get good reception. As the night draws nearer, they start to shiver and Paulie loses his shoe in the snow. They manage to find an abandoned van where they spend the rest of the night. Paulie rips up the van's carpet for blankets, and he and Christopher share ketchup packets for sustenance. When Christopher blames Paulie for the predicament and accuses him of trying to save himself at his expense, the two have an angry confrontation in an attempt to ascertain the true culprit. The morning after, they leave the van and try to retrace their steps.

Tony soon gets worried and asks Bobby Bacala to help him find them. Driving to the Barrens, Tony apologises for making fun of Bobby and expresses gratitude for his taking care of Junior. Arriving at the woods, they yell for a response. As they are walking, Paulie's makeshift shoe falls off and he shoots it in a fit of frustration. Tony and Bacala hear the shots start calling for Paulie and Christopher. They respond and soon meet up with each other. Paulie and Christopher are grateful they have been found and climb into Tony's Suburban, but Tony is clearly irritated with Paulie for getting himself in such a predicament, telling him to take responsibility for any trouble they have made.

During a session with Dr. Melfi, Tony tells her of his problems with Gloria who advises him that another woman in his life was equally "impossible to please". She then asks: "Does this remind you of any other woman?". After a thoughtful pause, Tony shakes his head.

Trivia

- *Terence Winter and Timothy Van Patten received an award from the Writers Guild of America for their work on this episode.

- As of the sixth season, the whereabouts of Valery, the Russian remain unknown

- In the DVD commentary for this episode, director Steve Buscemi has said that he was the one who threw the steak at Tony's head.

- Director Steve Buscemi played a character in Fargo who was also part of a two-man crew involved in taking a hostage.

- This episode was filmed at Harriman State Park in New York.

- The song played during the final montage/closing credits is the aria "Sposa Son Disprezzata" from the opera Bajazet by Antonio Vivaldi, sung by Cecilia Bartoli. It is about a wife who is scorned despite being faithful.

- The episode is widely considered to be one of the best ever by fans of the show.

"Amour Fou"

"Amour Fou" is the 38th episode of the HBO original series, The Sopranos. It was the 12th episode for the show's third season. The episode's teleplay was written by Frank Renzulli with a story idea from series creator, David Chase and was directed by Tim Van Patten. It originally aired on Sunday May 13, 2001.

Guest Starring

- Jason Cerbone as Jackie Aprile, Jr.
- Andrew Davoli as Dino Zerilli
- Louis Crugnali as Carlo Renzi
- Nick Tarabay as Matush
- Dan Grimaldi as Patsy Parisi
- Annabella Sciorra as Gloria Trillo
- Robert Funaro as Eugene Pontecorvo
- Toni Kalem as Angie Bonpensiero
- Sharon Angela as Rosalie Aprile
- Maureen Van Zandt as Gabriella Dante
- Richard Maldone as Ally Boy Barese

Synopsis

Carmela meets Meadow in an art gallery when she first begins spotting blood, and after excusing herself to the bathroom is brought to tears at the painting The Mystic Marriage of St. Catherine. Later, while watching a commercial on television, Carmela begins to sob over a dog food commercial. She then goes to confession and cops to meeting with a therapist on her own, and to fearing ovarian cancer. The priest advises her not to leave Tony, but to help him grow and to be more loving to him. Over lunch with the other mob wives, Rosalie tells them that they should all admire Hillary Clinton not for her distinguished career or for her intelligence, but for the way she handled herself when Bill Clinton admitted his affair. Carmela agrees, and pronounces Hillary as " an example to us all".

Tony continues to see Gloria even though she threw a London broil at his head. She apologizes to him in the parking lot of Melfi's office but Tony reminds her that if she were a guy "[he] wouldn't have to tell her where she would be right now". When he tells this to Dr. Melfi, she once again tells him that Gloria is a lot like Livia and attempts to help him draw parallels. Melfi then tells Tony that Gloria does love him and that she has a history of bad relationships, which Melfi cannot elaborate on. Tony decides to give the relationship another chance, but when Gloria blames Tony for slashing her tires, and meets Carmela the following day at Globe Motors, he calls the relationship quits. During a heated argument with Gloria, she mockingly asks if she should just act like a mute, and says a few other phrases that Livia had said to Tony more than once. He suddenly realizes that Melfi is right, that she is exactly like his mother. When he goes for the door, Gloria threatens to tell Carmela and Meadow about the affair if he leaves. He then punches her and begins to choke her. She begs him to kill her, further cementing her resemblance to Livia as she had begged for death several times in a dramatic and grandiose fashion, but he leaves instead. The following day, Patsy Parisi takes a test drive on one of the models with Gloria. Patsy then warns Gloria that if she goes near Tony Soprano again or tries to contact him or his family, "they will be scraping your nipples from these fine leather seats" and that he, not Tony, will be the one who murders her.

Meanwhile, Jackie Jr. and his friend Dino want to become more than associates. After hearing Ralphie's story of how Tony and Jackie Sr. got on an accelerated path to getting made after robbing Feech La Manna's card game, Jackie and Dino plan to execute a copycat manuever during Gene Pontecervo's game. At first, Jackie and Dino chicken out and decide to stay home and watch movies, but later that evening they change their minds again, and invite Carlo Renzi because he has a shotgun. They head for the Aprile crew hangout where the poker game is taking place, but are momentarily unnerved when the players consist of familiar faces: Christopher, Furio, and Ally Boy Barese. Carlo and Dino demand the money while Jackie stays silent for fear they will know his voice. The dealer, Sunshine, keeps advising the boys to leave, and soon, Dino panics and shoots him. As the mobsters draw guns, a firefight breaks out; Jackie shoots Furio in the thigh, and Christopher shoots Carlo in the forehead while Jackie and Dino flee into the street. Matush, Jackie's getaway driver who had in the past been beaten by Christopher for selling drugs at the Crazy Horse, abandoned ship when he got wind of the gunshots, took off. Jackie hijacks a passing car, deserting Dino, who is caught and killed by Ally Boy and Christopher. Furio is then rushed to the office of Dr. Fried, who, as it turns out, is a specialist not in gunshot wounds but in erectile dysfunction. In the waiting room, Christopher tells Tony that he knows Jackie Jr. was the escaped robber and that he has to be killed. Tony yells at Christopher that he will be respected and he will decide what happens

At the pork store the following morning, Ralphie meets Tony. Ralphie desperately wants to give Jackie Jr a pass because he is his girlfriend Rosalie's son, but he cannot take the events of the poker game lightly. Tony tells Ralphie that since Pontecorvo is a member of Ralphie's crew, it is his decision, and that although he will understand if Ralphie gives Jackie Jr. a pass, the other captains' respect for him might wane. Ralphie later tells Rosalie that Jackie probably went to Florida, and that he has a substance abuse problem, which deeply upsets her.

Hits

- Sunshine: a card dealer for the mob who was shot during the poker robbery.
- Carlo Renzi: shot by Christopher during the poker

robbery.
- Dino Zerilli: shot outside of the Aprile hangout by Christopher and Eugene Ally Boy Barese.

Trivia

- Ralph retells to Jackie and Dino the story about Jackie Sr. and Tony robbing the card game of "Feech La Manna" who ran the game every Saturday night, revealing that he was supposed to go along with them, and that the robbery put Jackie and Tony on the fast track to being made.

- The opening song "Sposa Son Disprezzata" as sung by Cecilia Bartoli was used during the closing montage/credits in the previous episode "Pine Barrens".

- The working title for this episode was "Stepping Up".

- The shell casings which can be seen striking the pavement after Chris executes Dino outside the card game were added into the scene in post-production

"Army of One'

"Army of One" is the 39th episode of the HBO original series, The Sopranos. It was the 13th episode for the show's third season. The episode was written by David Chase and Lawrence Konner and was directed by John Patterson. It originally aired on Sunday May 20, 2001.

Guest Starring

- Jason Cerbone as Jackie Aprile, Jr.
- Dan Grimaldi as Patsy Parisi
- Vince Curatola as Johnny Sack
- Joseph R. Gannascoli as Vito Spatafore
- Lola Glaudini as Agent Deborah Ciccerone
- Sharon Angela as Rosalie Aprile
- Maureen Van Zandt as Gabriella Dante
- Denise Borino as Ginny Sacrimoni
- Tobin Bell as Major Zwingli
- Frank Pellegrino as Bureau Chief Frank Cubitoso
- Matt Servitto as Agent Dwight Harris
- Frank Pando as Agent Grasso
- Melissa Marsala as Kelli Aprile

Synopsis

Jackie Jr, fearing execution at the hands of the mob, hides in the projects in Bontoon, calling Tony so they can settle the matter before he gets killed. Tony tells him to stay where he is, but to talk to Ralphie, who is making the final call. Tony then meets Ralphie, who has been hesitating over his judgement of Jackie, and asks that he make his decision in a "timely fashion". As it turns out, Ralphie has made up his mind, and had already dispatched Vito Spatafore to find Jackie. When Jackie leaves the apartment to get some air, Vito shoots him in the back of the head and leaves him lying in the snow, dead.

Meanwhile, Anthony Jr. and another friend confess to cheating on a geometry test after their principal tricks them by convincing them he has uncovered DNA evidence at the scene of the crime, and A.J. is promptly expelled from Verbum Dei. Tony becomes extremely angered when he hears the news and decides to send A.J. to military school before it's too late and his son is lost. Over dinner, Tony and Carmela mull over school brochures, and A.J. nervously waits for them to come to a decision as to what to do with him. Carmela then receives a phone call from Marie, Rosalie's sister, informing her that Jackie was shot and killed by "drug dealers". Carmela then hurries over to Rosalie's to comfort her.

At a sitdown with Paulie Walnuts, Tony and Ralphie, Paulie states that because he gave Ralph the combination to a safe that the Aprile crew later robbed, he is owed half of the take ($50,000). Tony listens to the case and rules that Ralphie turn over $12,000, to Paulie's disappointment. When Paulie tries to convince Tony to rethink his decision, Silvio states that Tony has made the decision and the sitdown is over.

Uncle Junior's cancer is in remission, leaving him physically competent for a RICO trial. However, the FBI has bigger fish to fry and is still intent on bringing down Tony Soprano. With Pussy Bonpensiero M.I.A. (hit), Agent Harris recommends that they get to Tony through Christopher Moltisanti, and get to him through Adriana. Bureau Chief Frank Cubitoso enlists Agent Deborah Ciccerone on an mission to work undercover and befriend Chris's fiancée, Adriana, and report back on whatever information she can get.

Later, A.J. is taken to an appointment with the military school's principal, Major Zwingli, who lays out the basic expectations and the schedules of the new recruits. Zwingli then has a talk with Tony and Carmela about the rigorous program and how he believes it will benefit their child. Carmela is still a little concerned since she believes they are training him to be a killer, but Tony feels that their son would be learning discipline, not violence.

At Jackie's wake, Rosalie and her daughter Kelli are, of course, extremely emotional, however, when Meadow sees Jackie lying in his casket she begins to sob uncontrollably. Tony and Carmela try to comfort her, but are further embarrassed when Rosalie notes that since the funeral is on Super Bowl Sunday, attendance is low. When everyone settles down, Carmela views Jackie lying in his casket and decides that maybe military school is best for AJ after all.

As A.J. prepares to depart for the academy, he puts on his dress uniform for his parents. Carmela and Tony are beaming with pride, but A.J. is humiliated and, in tears, asks not to be sent away. Tony is dismissive and assures A.J. that the decision has already been made, AJ needs to toughen up and accept it. A.J. promptly suffers a panic attack and collapses. In therapy, Tony relates events to Dr. Melfi, and beside himself that A.J. has inherited his psychiatric affliction, says that he can no longer send his son to military school. He says he is beginning to lose hope that he can ever rescue his child from disaster.

While Jackie Jr is being laid to rest, Christopher and Silvio are arrested for illegal gambling at the cemetery and are escorted to the District Attorney's office, while Paulie flees through the headstones. Uncle Junior witnesses this and runs back to his car, nearly leaving Bobby Bacala behind. After the burial, a small group of people return to Rosalie's to comfort her before proceeding to Vesuvio's. At the restaurant car park, Paulie meets Johnny Sack, and expresses his contempt for Tony's ruling in Ralphie's favour, telling Johnny to try and work for the New York family boss, Carmine Lupertazzi. Back inside, Junior begins to sing a sentimental Italian love songs and Meadow angrily throws pieces of bread at her grand-uncle Junior as he sings. Confronted by her father outside, Meadow tearfully denounces the funeral proceedings as "bullshit" and runs across the street, narrowly avoiding being hit by a car. Tony returns to the dinner, quietly telling Carmela that Meadow hopefully has money to catch a ride back to Columbia. He then puts his arms around A.J. as they listen to Uncle Junior sing.

Hits

- Jackie Aprile, Jr.: murdered by Vito Spatafore near the Boonton housing projects

Trivia

- In the original 2001 broadcast, Agent Deborah Ciccerone was played by actress Fairuza Balk. However due to scheduling conflicts, she was not able to return for Season 4. For the DVD recordings and future repeats of the episode, shots of Balk were replaced with Lola Glaudini, who went on to replace Balk permanently in 2002.

- Vito and Jackie Jr. are cousins as Ritchie Aprile was an uncle to them both. Also, when Bryan Spatafore (Vito's brother) was injured in the episode "Another Toothpick", Jackie Jr. said that Bryan was his cousin. However we never see Vito or Jackie Jr. mentioning each other as cousins, nor do we see the former contemplating over the murder of a family member.

- During Jackie's wake, Uncle Junior's performance of "Core 'ngrato" ("Ungrateful Heart") was actually sung by Dominic Chianese.

The Sopranos:

Season Four

"For All Debts Public and Private"

"For All Debts Public and Private" is the 40th episode of the HBO original series, The Sopranos. It was the 1st episode for the show's fourth season. The episode was written by David Chase and was directed by Allen Coulter. It originally aired on September 15, 2002

Guest Starring

- Tom Mason as Detective Lieutenant Barry Haydu
- Tom Aldredge as Hugh DeAngelis
- Sharon Angela as Rosalie Aprile
- Will Arnett as Agent Mike Waldrup
- Val Bisoglio as Murf Lupo
- Joseph R. Gannascoli as Vito Spatafore
- Lola Glaudini as Agent Deborah Ciccerone/Danielle Ciccolella
- Dan Grimaldi as Patsy Parisi
- Toni Kalem as Angie Bonpensiero
- Marianne Leone as Joanne Moltisanti
- Tony Lip as Carmine Lupertazzi
- George Loros as Raymond Curto
- Richard Maldone as Albert Barese
- Angelo Massagli as Bobby Baccalieri, Jr.
- Arthur J. Nascarella as Carlo Gervasi
- Christine Pedi as Karen Baccalieri

- Peter Riegert as Assemblyman Ronald Zellman
- Frank Santorelli as Georgie
- Suzanne Shepherd as Mary DeAngelis
- Lexie Sperduto as Sophia Baccalieri
- Matthew Sussman as Dr. Douglas Schreck
- Gay Thomas-Wilson as Nurse - Dr. Schreck's office (probable FBI agent)

Synopsis

AJ Soprano has started in a new school and Carmella is trying to contribute to his enrichment by reading to him from the New York Times. Tony also asks about his grades, event hough he's only three days into the semester. Carmela's mood visibly brightens when Tony's driver arrives, but her smile fades when she sees it is Christopher instead of Furio, seeing as she has accidentally developed a little crush on the latter.

Tony and Uncle Junior continue to get together while still adhering to the boundaries of Junior's house arrest by meeting in the office of Dr. Schreck - Junior's physician. Chris, Bobby Bacala and Murf Lupo wait for them outside, all flirting with a nurse that works there. In the meeting with Tony, Junior says he needs more to cover his mounting legal costs. Tony tells him there is little enough to go around and angrily refuses to help, advocatig that he get his "shy running right" before asking again. Junior later decides to demote aging capo Murf and replace him with Bobby Baccala, which Tony approves of. These meetings, however, quickly come to an end when Junior's lawyer tells Murf the FBI has placed an agent in Dr Schreck's office in the guise of a nurse.

Tony later has Chris take him to the Bada Bing where he vents his frustration by beating up Georgie the bartender for wasting ice. Silvio had tried to defuse the situation but failed. Chris, Sil and Tony depart the Bing on foot to attend a meeting with the family's Capos - Carlo Gervasi, Albert Barese, Ray Curto and Ralph Cifaretto. Tony uses the meeting to harangue them about the near-negative growth in the family's business, telling them Junior desperately needs their support. Christopher is left outside with Vito Spatafore while the senior family members have their discussion.

Chris believes his return to driver status may be a slap on the wrist for questioning Tony's judgement about the Jackie Jr. situation, and when he returns home he discusses this with Adriana. Adriana still has her friend Danielle over, and Christopher is rude to her. Christopher also seems to have developed a serious drug habit although he insists he is just "chipping", shooting heroin every day and trying to get Adriana to join him.

Carmela notices widow Angie Bonpensiero working in a supermarket and does not approach her. This encounter with the widow of a former mobster who doesnt seem to be getting any help prompts Carmela to worry about her financial security should anything happen to Tony, and when she asks Tony for money so she can make an investment he tells her there is no longer money kept in the house. He is then shown removing cash from his car and putting it under a floor tile in the pool house. Later in the episode Tony buys bags of duck feed so he can store cash in the bags. Carmela notices that it is an odd time to buy duck feed. While out buying the feed Tony meets with Assemblyman Zellman to discuss the Esplanade project and talk property - Zellman tips him that prices near the new development are likely to see a big jump, and Tony remembers that Junior owns a warehouse in the that area.

Carmela invites Rosalie and Ralph Cifaretto over for dinner despite Tony's requests that she not do so. Rosalie is withdrawn and quiet, but Ralph is animated and full of conversation. Ralphie excuses himself to use the bathroom and Janice soon follows him and they end up doing coke and having sex in the bathroom. During the dinner Adriana brings over her friend Danielle, who, unbeknownst to her is an FBI agent working under cover, and using a separate phone line that she reserves just for Adriana's calls. Adriana is there to borrow something from Carmela, and while they talk Tony flirts with Danielle, and Rosalie then shows her around the Soprano house. Meadow, still greiving over Jackie's death, is not at dinner and still has not signed up for fall classes at Columbia despite the fact that summer is rapidly coming to a close.

Later, Tony meets with Carmine Luptertazzi, he has a party in a hotel room, hosting Christopher, Ralphie, Silvio and a number of Icelandic air stewardesses also attend. Chris smokes heroin in the bathroom with one of the girls until Tony pulls him out, asking him to come with him somewhere. They meet Bobby Bacala at a diner, and while there, Tonyhe tells Christopher he knows who killed his father - Detective Lt. Barry Haydu. Chris recalls that he had been told it was a police officer that killed his father but he believed that the man was already dead. Tony gives Chris Haydu's address and wishes him luck. Tony and Bobby then leave Chris to pursue his new prey.

Chris reaches Haydu's home and breaks into his house. When Haydu arrives home from from his retirement party, Chris knocks him unconscious, taking his gun and his badge and handcuffing him to the stairway. When Haydu comes around Chris questions him about his involvement with his father's death and Haydu denies everything. Chris tells him it doesn't matter what he says because Tony wants him killed. He turns up the volume on the TV, shoots Haydu, shoots up the house, wipes the gun with a bill from Haydu's own wallet, and places the gun in Haydu's hand. Chris later goes to visit his mother, Joanne, and pins the twenty dollars he took from Haydu to his mother's fridge.

While Chris is pursuing Haydu, Bobby and Tony eat dinner and discuss Bobby's promotion and how he has coped with his own father's death. Bobby and Tony visit Junior's house early the next morning learns of the situation with the nurse in Dr Schreck's office. Tony offers Junior a hundred thousand for his warehouse, telling him it is to help with his financial difficulties. Junior accepts the offer but is despondent and appears to have given up hope, telling Tony he is an old man who is going to trial.

Meanwhile Paulie has been arrested in Youngstown, Ohio. He calls Johnny Sack and explains that he was visiting a friend, Lenny Scortese, and they got caught with a gun from an unsolved homicide in their car. John seems keen to cultivate his friendship with Paulie.

In therapy Tony discusses Carmela pressuring him over the family's future and Uncle Junior's life. When Tony discusses his future in terms of two endings, death or prison, Dr. Melfi urges him to give up the business. Tony tells her that he has a plan to avoid both - using Christopher as an intermediary to distance himself from any repercussions. Dr. Melfi questions Tony's frankness and he tells her that he trusts her…sort of.

First Appearances

- Bobby Baccalieri, Jr.: Bobby's son
- Karen Baccalieri: Bobby's wife
- Sophia Baccalieri: Bobby's daughter
- Carlo Gervasi: Soprano/DiMeo crime family capo
- Murf Lupo: Ageing Soprano/DiMeo crime family capo and friend of Junior Soprano

Hits

- Det. Lt. Barry Haydu: murdered in his home by Christopher Moltisanti

Trivia

- The song in the closing credits is "World Destruction" by Time Zone.

- Vince Curatola (Johnny Sack) is now billed in the opening credits.

- Paulie's prison stay was written in order to allow more time off for actor Tony Sirico who was recovering from major back surgery.

- The wrestler Johnny Valiant appears in this episode as Carmine Lupertazzi's bodyguard.

- Junior is shown watching the movie Heaven Knows, Mr. Allison with Deborah Kerr and Robert Mitchum

- At Lt. Haydu's house Chris is shown watching Magnum PI.

- This episode was the first one to be aired after

September 11. From this episode on, the shot of the World Trade Center Towers in the opening credits are gone.

"No Show"

"No Show" is the 41st episode of the HBO original series, The Sopranos. It was the 2nd episode for the show's fourth season. The episode was written by David Chase and Terence Winter and was directed by John Patterson. It originally aired on September 22, 2002.

Guest Starring

- Will Arnett as Agent Mike Waldrup
- Carl Capotorto as Little Paulie Germani
- Max Casella as Benny Fazio
- Robert Desiderio as Jack Massarone
- Raymond Franza as Donny K
- Danyelle Freeman as Misty Giaculo
- Robert Funaro as Eugene Pontecorvo
- Joseph R. Gannascoli as Vito Spatafore
- Lola Glaudini as Agent Deborah Ciccerone/Danielle Ciccolella
- Dan Grimaldi as Patsy Parisi
- Linda Lavin as Dr. Wendy Kobler
- George Loros as Raymond Curto
- Richard Maldone as Albert Barese
- Arthur J. Nascarella as Carlo Gervasi
- Frank Pellegrino as Chief Frank Cubitoso

- Matt Servitto as Agent Dwight Harris

Synopsis

Carmela tries to talk to Meadow about her failure to register for classes but Meadow again uses Jackie Jr.'s death as an excuse. She eventually tells her mother that she hasn't registered because she hopes to travel to Europe with her friend Misty. Tony consults with Dr. Melfi, and she recommends a psychiatrist specializing in adolescents. Meadow agrees to see Dr. Kobler, but Dr. Kobler actually encourages her to go to Europe with Misty. This prompts a protracted family argument where Meadow calls her father Mr Mob Boss. Tony responds by telling her he did everything he could to save Jackie Jr. She flees the house saying she has made up her mind, eventually going to Columbia and registering while her parents worry she has left the country.

Carmela's friendship with Furio continues and she continues to take pleasure in his morning visits to pick up Tony, and he in turn confides that he is buying a house.

The crew throw a birthday party for Albert Barese at Vesuvio. Ralphie makes joke about Ginny Sack's weight - saying she has had a 95 pound mole removed from her ass. While Paulie is incarcerated Patsy and Little Paulie have arranged a sit down on his behalf to discuss Ralphie's division of jobs at the esplanade site. After some haggling they settle with five jobs - three no works and two no shows. As capo Paulie receives the first no show job, Silvio announces that Tony wants Christopher as acting capo of Paulie's crew during his absence and gives Chris the second no show job. Patsy is upset as he has been made longer, and it actually was Patsy and not Christopher who negotiated the jobs in the meeting.

As they leave the meeting Chris's jokes fall on deaf ears as Silvio privately fumes that Chris is beginning to usurp his role in Tony's life. Chris later visits the construction site where Patsy, Benny Fazio, Little Paulie, Donny K and Vito are enjoying their no work jobs, and Chris's interest is piqued when they mention to him that there is a lot of valuable materials floating around.

When the materials go missing Tony immediately calls Chris in to reprimand him. Tony tells him he is not seeing the financial potential of the construction contracts and is angry about the attention that petty thefts will bring. Christopher goes home to get high and complain to Adriana. He also relays the rebuke to crew members Patsy and Little Paulie but Patsy insists Chris gave him a look that he took as a go ahead.

Later Silvio complains to Tony that Patsy feels marginalized by Chris' promotion, but Tony is unpreturbed. Patsy then visits Silvio at the Bing and mentions some floor tiles at the site - Silvio tells him to steal them in spite of Tony's orders. Following this theft Jack Massarone finds Tony playing golf with Artie Bucco and tells him about what has happened, and Tony treats Chris to a vituperative diatribe for not effectively managing his crew and keeping them out of trouble. He drives straight to the Esplanade to confront Patsy and the argument descends into violence.

When a construction worker threatens to phone the police Patsy beats him with a scaffolding pole.

Adrianna, meanwhile, is meeting her friend Danielle at the Crazy Horse. When they meet Adriana discusses her fears that she may be unable to have children because of complications of an abortion she had before she was with Christopher. Danielle is sympathetic and gives her the name of an OB/GYN. Chris and Little Paulie arrive at the club and Chris gives Little Paulie cocaine in front of Danielle.

Ralphie and Janice's relationship continues and they are spending more and more time at Janice's house. Tony arrives unexpectedly and Ralphie hides upstairs but Tony finds his shoe and warns Janice about him. Little Paulie visits his Uncle in Youngstown and gives him the news from the sitdown. Paulie asks if anyone has been to visit his ma and Little Paulie tells him no-one has but that Tony sent a box of chocolates.

While Christopher, Adriana, and Danielle hang out at the Crazy Horse, Christopher kisses Adriana and puts a hand on Danielle's thigh. Danielle leaves and Adrianna and Chris argue: Chris claims Danielle put his hand on her thigh and Adriana chooses to believe him, and stop returning Danielle's calls. The FBI decides to bring Adriana in and reveal Danielle's true identity - Special Agent Deborah Ciccerone. Agent Harris accompanies agent Ciccerone to pick up Adriana. She is taken to meet with Chief Cubitoso where the agents tell her she can choose between 25 years in prison for possession and intent to supply (with an additional consequence of being responsible for bringing an undercover agent to the club and the homes of Tony Soprano and Moltisanti) or begin co-operating with them. Adriana, overwhelmed at these opportunities, throws up all over the table and Chief Cubitoso.

Trivia

- The episode creates a major plotline in the season regarding Ralphie's behavior.

- "Kid A" from Radiohead's Kid A album plays over the closing credits. This refers to Meadow, who plays a large role in this episode, as being the first born child, or "Kid A".

- When Christopher and Adriana are arguing at the Crazy Horse after the incident with Danielle, on one cut of Christopher, the couch is wet, the next cut the couch is dry, and wet again in the subsequent shot.

"Christopher"

"Christopher" is the 42nd episode of the HBO original series, The Sopranos. It was the 3rd episode for the show's fourth season. The episode's teleplay was written by Michael Imperioli, with a story idea by Imperioli and Maria Laurino and was directed by Tim Van Patten. It originally aired on September 29, 2002.
Contents

Guest Starring

- Jerry Adler as Hesh Rabkin
- Max Casella as Benny Fazio
- Sharon Angela as Rosalie Aprile
- Carl Capotorto as Little Paulie Germani
- Arthur Nascarella as Carlo Gervasi
- Paul Schulze as Father Phil Intintola
- Larry Sellers as Del Redclay
- Joyce Van Patten as Sandy
- Lola Glaudini as Agent Deborah Ciccerone
- Peter Riegert as Assemblyman Ronald Zellman
- Tony Lip as Carmine Lupertazzi
- Matt Servitto as Agent Harris
- Christine Pedi as Karen Baccalieri
- Montel Williams as Himself
- Richard Romanus as Richard La Penna

- Maureen Van Zandt as Gabriella Dante

Synopsis

Silvio decides to take action against Native American groups' protests of the Columbus Day Parade. Without Tony's approval, Silvio and Artie Bucco, along with a few other soldiers, threaten demonstrators not to burn an effigy of Columbus. As they leave after being warned by the police, Artie Bucco has a glass bottle thrown at him and several other soldiers are injured. Tony learns about this and blames Silvio for intervening. Ralphie meanwhile tries to threaten the protest leader, Del Redclay, to reconsider his stance on Columbus day, and Tony tries to dissolve the situation trying to get an Indian chief to convince Redclay not to protest during the parade. The chief is not particularly receptive to this idea, however, he invites Tony and his crew to his casino to gamble. While this sounds like a positive development, it means that the group got sidetracked, and both the parade and protest occur without mob intervention, which irritates Silvio.

Meanwhile at a luncheon meant to enforce Italian American Women's pride,, the "mob wives" are singled out (especially Carmela), when the speaker discusses the stereotypes of being an Italian. After the luncheon, Gabriella Dante lectures Father Intintola on how much Carmela Soprano has done for to the church, and that he had no right to bring in a guest speaker whose whole program was to judge and shame them about how their husbands make a living.

Paulie Walnuts begins to create tension between the families when he tells Johnny Sack about the joke involving Ginny Sack's 95 pound mole, and how Tony sold Uncle Junior's warehouse on Frelinghuysen Ave near the Riverfront Esplanade. Johnny Sack contacts Tony and demands a share of the profit since both crime families share the Esplanade and that it would be only fair if they shared the profit.

Shortly after, Karan Bacala dies in a car accident. At the wake, Bobby kneels near her casket and loudly sobs. The wives have pity on Bobby since he is rumored to have never taken a comare.

Janice Soprano continues to see Ralphie Cifaretto on the sly; however, after spending time with the newly widowed Bobby, she breaks up with Ralphie by violently throwing him down the stairs.

"The Weight"

"The Weight" is the 43rd episode of the HBO original series, The Sopranos. It was the 4th episode for the show's fourth season. The episode was written by Terence Winter and directed by Jack Bender. It originally aired on October 6, 2002.

Guest Starring

- Dan Grimaldi as Patsy Parisi
- Joseph R. Gannascoli as Vito Spatafore
- Carl Capotorto as Little Paulie Germani
- Peter Bogdanovich as Dr. Eliott Kupferberg
- Tony Lip as Carmine Lupertazzi
- Richard Maldone as Ally Boy Barese
- Robert Funaro as Eugene Pontecorvo
- Joe Maruzzo as Joe Peeps
- Sharon Angela as Rosalie Aprile
- Maureen Van Zandt as Gabriella Dante
- Matthew Del Negro as Brian Cammarata
- Denise Borino as Ginny Sacrimoni

Synopsis

While having dinner, Johnny Sack his New York associate Joe Peeps see Donny K, a member of Ralph Cifaretto's crew, joking with the barman, reminding him that Ralph had made an insulting joke about Ginny's weight. As Donny K. gets up to leave, Johnny follows him outside, beats him, and pees on him. When Tony hears of what happened, he is deeply disturbed by Johnny's behavior. Johnny complains to Tony about Ralph's joke, and while Tony agrees the joke is disgraceful and inappropriate, Ralph is one of his highest earners and must be protected.

Johnny then tries to convince Carmine and Uncle Junior to intervene in order to make a settlement since it may threaten the two families' already tense relationship regarding the Esplanade. Uncle Junior thinks that Johnny should receive a cut of the Aprile construction business but Johnny is pushing for Ralph to be whacked for disrespecting his wife. After failing to gain support from first Tony and then Carmine and Junior, Johnny decides to order a hit on Ralphie while he is vacationing in Miami. Meanwhile, Carmine, concerned about Esplanade profits in the wake of the situation, makes a veiled suggestion to Tony to have his underboss killed. Uncle Junior suggets to Tony that he should to put a hit on Johnny via an elderly soldier from Rhode Island, Lou "DiMaggio" Galina. In Miami, however, an assassin traces Ralph to his hotel.

Back in Jersey, Johnny catches Ginny in their laundry room stuffing her face with junk food and yells at her for bringing so much shame upon him with her overly generous stature. Ginny gets upset and tries to convince Johnny that she wants to lose weight, but Johnny has a change of heart and assures her he does not care about how she looks as long as she is happy. His anger subsiding, he calls off the hit on Ralphie at the last second and approaches Tony, offering reconciliation. Surprised, but relieved, Tony calls off the hit on Johnny.

Meanwhile, Meadow is recommended by Elliott Kupferberg's daughter Saskia to join the South Bronx Law Center. Tony thinks this is a terrible idea, however, given that the South Bronx Law Center primarily serves underprivileged clients and the position will not be lucrative. Meadow, however, volunteers anyway. Meanwhile, Carmela draws emotionally closer to Furio, who throws a housewarming party to celebrate his new home, and the pair dance alone to Italian music. Carmela is happy that Furio is staying permanently and takes along an unsuspecting A.J. as a sort of a chaperone when she goes to Furio's home to help him decorate.

The following evening as Tony and Carmela lay in bed, Tony presents Carmela with a slim designer dress which he then asks her to put on. Carmela does so and Tony tenderly compliments her model figure. They begin to make love as Meadow plays music inthe next room, reminding Carmela of Furio.

Trivia

- The title refers to the joke Ralph Cifaretto made about Ginny Sacrimoni's weight in "No Show" which Johnny Sack eventually learned about.

- Music from Furio's housewarming includes "O'Mare" by the Italian band, Spaccanapoli and "Vesuvio" by Angelo De Falco.

"Pie-O-My"

"Pie-O-My" is the 44th episode of the HBO original series, The Sopranos. It was the fifth episode for the show's fourth season. The episode was written by Robin Green & Mitchell Burgess and directed by Henry J. Bronchtein. It originally aired on Sunday October 13, 2002.

Guest Starring

- Jerry Adler as Hesh Rabkin
- Dan Grimaldi as Patsy Parisi
- Tony Darrow as Larry Boy Barese
- Joseph R. Gannascoli as Vito Spatafore
- Arthur J. Nascarella as Carlo Gervasi
- Robert Funaro as Eugene Pontecorvo
- Richard Portnow as Harold Melvoin
- Matt Servitto as Agent Harris
- Karen Young as Agent Sanseverino
- Lola Glaudini as Agent Deborah Ciccerone
- Matthew Del Negro as Brian Cammarata
- Michele Santopietro as JoJo Palmice

Synopsis

After Ralph buys a racehorse named "Pie-O-My," she wins a couple races and makes a lot of money for Ralph and Tony. Ralph gives Tony some of the winnings because the mob boss picked the strategy for the winning races. Tony, always drawn to animals, grows fond of the horse, while Ralph on the other hand orders the trainer to "tell that midget to not go easy with the whip".

Carmela asks Tony to invest in a stock and sign papers for a life insurance trust, but Tony's accountant advises against it because the advantages go to Carmela if Tony dies. Once Tony relents on the stock and tells her to buy, she angrily tells him that it has been split and they missed the chance.

Janice, meanwhile, still has an interest in Bobby. She interferes in a conversation between him and JoJo Palmice, and then gives the dinner JoJo had made for Bobby to Junior. Janice also takes credit for Carmela's lasagna and tries to get Bobby to focus on his work. After Janice tells him Junior is counting on him, Bobby manages to strongarm a union representative into changing his vote in an upcoming election.

With medical bills for Pie-O-My cutting into her winnings, Ralph refuses to call the vet one night when the horse becomes sick and needs help. Once word gets to Tony, he rushes to the stables and pays the vet, telling him he better hope the horse "makes it." He then goes into the stall and strokes the horse's neck, telling her everything will be all right.

Trivia

- At the stables, Hesh references Seabiscuit who was at the time a frequent pop culture reference due to the popularity of the book about him.

- The closing song is "My Rifle, My Pony and Me" by Dean Martin.

"Everybody Hurts"

"Everybody Hurts" is the 45th episode of the HBO original series, The Sopranos. It was the sixth episode for the show's fourth season. The episode was written by Michael Imperioli and directed by Steve Buscemi. It originally aired on Sunday October 20, 2002.

Guest Starring

- Joseph R. Gannascoli as Vito Spatafore
- Matthew Del Negro as Brian Cammarata
- Heidi Dippold as Janelle Cammarata
- Lauren Toub as Liz DiLiberto
- Murielle Arden as Elodie Colbert
- Jean-Hugues Anglade as Jean-Philippe Colbert
- Jessica Dunphy as Devin Pillsbury
- Paul Dano as Patrick Whalen
- Cameron Boyd as Matt Testa
- Ryan Hoffman as Jason Malatesta
- Annabella Sciorra as Gloria Trillo

Synopsis

Christopher, still shooting up, is sinking into sleep as he finishes a hit, jarred awake by a call from Tony, who wants to see him.

When Chris arrives Tony notices that he is a little out of it, but Chris passes it off as the effects of too much wine. Tony tells Chris that he is going to be giving orders through him in the future because of their family ties, and that Chris will take the family into the 21st century. Chris points out that the 21st century has already arrived, but Tony doesn't seem to follow.

A.J. hangs out with his friends Matt Testa, Patrick Whalen and Jason Malatesta and girlfriend Devin Pillsbury in a basement, and when he tells them that his father co-owns the Bada Bing! they decide to visit. Unfortunately AJ gets confused and they end up at Satriale's. AJ comes home late and his mother scolds him for being out past his curfew.

In bed, Tony and Carmela discuss Furio Giunta - she wants to see if he'd hit it off with her dental hygienist Liz DiLiberto. She also tells him that she has learned that Gloria Trillo killed herself. Tony can barely conceal his shock, angrily confronting Dr. Melfi in therapy - blaming her for Gloria's death. She stands up to him and informs him she gives her patients everything, and that this can't be blamed on her anymore than it could be blamed on him. Tony relents and admits that he is actually feeling guilty himself since he cut off their relationship, and has displaced his anger by accusing Melfi of giving poor care.

Artie Bucco has a new hostess at Nuovo Vesuvio, a French girl named Elodie, and his relationship with Charmaine seems even more strained. Elodie's brother also has asked Artie if he could borrow money to buy distribution rights for Armagnac - he claims it is the new vodka. Artie is sucked in by the deal and goes to borrow money from Ralphie but Ralphie refuses because he would not be able to muscle Artie if he did not pay him back. Later Tony learns of this and visits Artie at home, offering the money himself and says he upset that Artie didn't come to him first.

Tony drinks from a bottle of Armagnac and has a drunken dream about Gloria. He visits her apartment and finds her wearing a black dress and a black scarf. She is cooking dinner for him, and as she does some the scarf drapes across Tony. Plaster falls down in front of him and when he looks up at the ceiling he sees that the chandelier is almost pulled out. Gloria is suddenly back at the table and offers Tony a choice between seeing what she has under her dress or under her scarf. Tony awakens and makes his way to the bathroom for some medication.

Brian visits the Sopranos and Tony signs the new trust papers. Tony also puts Brian in touch with Patsy as he spots his taste for good tailoring. Later AJ and his girlfriend Devin are interrupted by Carmela while making out on the sofa, using a car service to drive to see Meadow in order to ask if they can borrow her room while she is volunteering in the Bronx. They are shocked at the neighbourhood that Meadow volunteers in and disappointed when she laughs off their request.

Tony continues his string of good deeds by putting together a night at a Billy Joel concert for Carmela, Chris, Adriana, Brian and his wife Janelle. Adriana flakes - afraid of spending too much time with the people she is supposed to be collecting evidence about. This makes way for Carmela to set up Furio and Liz, although once they are there she seems less than happy with her match-making. He also books a dinner with Janice at Nuovo Vesuvio. Tony congratulates Janice on her relationship with Bobby. Janice responds by telling Tony what he needed to hear - he always reaches out to her when it counts.

Artie delivers Tony's money to Jean-Philippe outside Vesuvio. Later, he is unable to get hold of him and Elodie distracts him by flirting with him. Artie eventually decides to visit Jean-Philippe at home, prepping himself in the mirror and rehearsing the conversation on the way. It goes badly and they end up fighting - Jean-Philippe rips out Artie's new ear-ring and throws him out. Artie goes home and overdoses, and when he calls Tony, Tony phones an ambulance and visits Artie in the hospital - he is angry for Artie's actions but assumes the Elodie's brother's debt so that Artie won't owe him money. Later in therapy he tells Dr. Melfi about Artie and then of his decision to put it behind him by donating money to the suicide hotline. Furio has a more successful meeting with Jean-Philippe than Artie did.

Trivia

- The title refers to the R.E.M. song of the same name about resisting the impulse to commit suicide in times of suffering.

- Elodi's Leopard print outfit reflects the fact that Adriana used to hold the hostess position.

- Dave Edmunds' Take me for a Little While plays over the end credits.

"Watching Too Much Television"

"Watching Too Much Television" is the 46th episode of the HBO original series, The Sopranos. It was the seventh episode for the show's fourth season. The episode's teleplay was written by Nick Santora and Terence Winter with a story by Robin Green & Mitchell Burgess, Terence Winter and David Chase and directed by John Patterson. It originally aired on Sunday October 27, 2002.

Guest Starring

- Richard Maldone as Albert "Ally Boy" Barese
- Joseph R. Gannascoli as Vito Spatafore
- Dan Grimaldi as Patsy Parisi
- Max Cassella as Benny Fazio
- Carl Capotorto as Little Paulie Germani
- Peter Riegert as Ronald Zellman
- Vondie Curtis-Hall as Maurice Tiffen
- Sharon Angela as Rosalie Aprile
- Maureen Van Zandt as Gabriella Dante
- Anna Mancini as Donna Parisi
- Patty McCormack as Liz LaCerva
- Marianne Leone as Joanne Moltisanti
- Matthew Del Negro as Brian Cammarata
- Lauren Toub as Liz DiLiberto
- Oksana Babiy as Irina Peltsin

- Richard Portnow as Harold Melvoin
- Lewis J Standlen as Dr. Ira Fried
- Frank Pellegrino as Bureau Chief Frank Cubitoso
- Matt Servito as Agent Dwight Harris
- Lola Glaudini as Agent Deborah Ciccerone Waldrup
- Karen Young as Agent Robyn Sanseverino

Synopsis

Paulie is released from prison and attends a huge party in his honor, hosted at the Bada Bing. Tony and Ralphie figure out the next day that they may be able to make a lot of money defrauding the HUD with bogus housing deals. Tony recruits Zellman and a friend of his, Maurice Tiffen, a one-time idealist and former head of a non-profit low income housing program, to put the plan into action. They also recruit Dr. Fried to initially purchase the property. Zellman confesses that he has started seeing Irina - Tony at first seems to approve, or at least, not to disapprove, but later his jealousy flares and he barges into Zellman's place and beats him with a belt in front of Irina.

Meanwhie, Adriana's covert meetings with FBI continue. Believing that the FBI will stop hassling her if they can't use her testimony, she pressures Christopher to finally set a date for their wedding. Later, during a casual conversation, she finds out that marital privilege may not benefit her after all. She secretly goes to a lawyer, who tells her that marital privilege will only apply to conversations that take place after they get married, are not in the presence of a third party, and do not further any criminal enterprise. Since every conversation she's ever had with Christopher violates at least one of these rules, marriage will not get her out of the mess she's found herself in. This is reinforced in a separate scene, where the FBI are indifferent to the idea of her marrying Christopher.

Elsewhere, Carmela and Furio's tentative flirtation continues as he calls her looking for his sunglasses. Paulie meets with the FBI for a meal and he divulges the HUD scheme while seeking assurance from Johnny that their discussions are private.

"Mergers and Acquisitions"

"Mergers and Acquisitions" is the 47th episode of the HBO original series, The Sopranos. It was the seventh episode for the show's fourth season. The episode's teleplay was written by Lawrence Konner with a story by Robin Green & Mitchell Burgess and Terence Winter and directed by Dan Attias. It originally aired on Sunday November 3, 2002.

Guest Starring

- Sharon Angela as Rosalie Aprile
- Fran Anthony as Minn Martone
- Leslie Bega as Valentina La Paz
- Anna Berger as Cookie Cirillo
- Carl Capotorto as Little Paulie Germani
- Max Casella as Benny Fazio
- Charlotte Colavin as Lorraine Cirillo
- Matthew Del Negro as Brian Cammarata
- Heidi Dippold as Janelle Cammarata
- Frances Ensemplare as Marianucci Gualtieri
- Dan Grimaldi as Patsy Parisi
- Anthony Patellis as Chuckie Cirillo
- Paul Schulze as Father Phil Intintola

Synopsis

Paulie is concerned about his mother's welfare when she moves into Green Grove. Upon arriving, Nucci is happy to reunite with old friends Cookie Cirillo and Minn Martone who warmly welcome her. However, when Nucci is in the restroom, the ladies politely and sweetly tell Paulie that Nucci will not be able to play cards with them or eat lunch together since they are a set group. Paulie insists that they make room and be respectful to his mother, but they don't seem to put much weight in his wishes. At Casino night, Nucci is treated as a pariah after ruining a blackjack game, then takes to confining herself to her room and causing Paulie significant worry. Paulie then pays a visit to Cookie's son Chuckie, who is a high school principal. Paulie talks to him about their mothers' friendship and feels that they are facing challenges due to the fact that Minn Martone is an instigator and a "malignant cunt". Chuckie tries to convince Paulie that he cannot intervene with who his mother is friends with since she is a grown women, but the following day Chuckie is chased through a hallway by members of Paulie's crew and is badly injured. When Chuckie's wife threatens to take Cookie out of the nursing home, Cookie reluctantly agrees to make peace with Nucci.

Meanwhile at the stables, Tony meets Ralph's girlfriend Valentina La Paz and Tony is immediately smitten. Valentina then convinces Tony to have a portrait made of him with Pie-O-My and after they sit for it, the two have sex. Valentina continues to date Ralph, and Tony buys her an expensive pin as a parting gift since he feels that their relationship cannot continue due to her relationship with Ralphie. Valentina, however, still wants to see him, and complains to Tony that her sex life with Ralph consists mostly of his masochistic fetishes. Dr. Melfi suggests that Tony is reluctant to "cuckold" Ralph, and in fact Tony continues to keep Valentina at arm's length until he gets confirmation from Janice, who has the inside scoop, that Ralph really does have a masochism fetish.

Carmela, who is falling for Furio, feels bad for Furio when he leaves for Italy to attend his father's funeral. While in Italy, Furio discusses his attraction to Carmela with his uncle, but his uncle warms him not pursue the relationship any further since it would be considered an act of treason to sleep with the boss' wife. At home, Carmela discovers a broken fake nail in Tony's clothes, infuriating her. She vents her anger by taking a stipend of money from his bird feed and investing it with several stock brokers. She then leaves the fake nail on the nightstand so there is no confusion about what she feels and why. Tony walks downstairs, where Carmela is reading the paper. He asks for coffee, which she makes, and asks Tony if he wishes to discuss anything. He says no. A.J. comes downstairs, and Tony, in a similar effort to prevent confusion, asks if A.J. had been through the bird feed, tipping off Carmela the he knows she's taken the money. After A.J. leaves, Carmela again asks Tony if he wishes to talk about anything. He declines, and asks Carmela the same -- she, as well, declines. The scene ends with Carmela sitting and reading the paper, Tony standing, and the coffee brewing.

First Appearances

- Valentina La Paz: An art dealer and Ralph's girlfriend who quickly begins to fall for Tony.

Hits

- Furio's Father: Cancer

Trivia

- The phrase mergers and acquisitions refers to the aspect of corporate finance strategy and management dealing with the merging and acquiring of different companies as well as other assets.

"Whoever did this"

"Whoever Did This" is the 48th episode of the HBO original series, The Sopranos. It was the ninth episode for the show's fourth season. The episode was written by Robin Green & Mitchell Burgess and directed by Tim Van Patten. It originally aired on Sunday 10 November 2002.

Guest Starring

- Joseph R. Gannascoli as Vito Spatafore
- Allia Kliouka Schaffer as Svetlana Kirilenko
- Sharon Angela as Rosalie Aprile
- Leslie Bega as Valentina LaPaz
- Dane Curley as Justin Cifaretto
- Marissa Matrone as Ronnie Capozza
- Richard D'Alessandro as Dennis Capozza
- Frances Ensemplare as Nucci Gualtieri
- Murielle Arden as Elodi Colbert
- Richard Portnow as Harold Melvoin
- Dan Castleman as Prosecutor Castleman
- Matt Servito as Agent Harris
- Frank Pando as Agent Grasso
- Paul Schulze as Father Phil Initintola

Synopsis

While playing an unsupervised game about Lord of the Rings, Ralphie's son Justin is hurt when an arrow strikes him in the chest and is lodged there, rendering him comatose with probable brain damage. At the hospital Ralphie is devastated and gets into an argument with his ex-wife Ronnie. Overwhelmed by guilt, Ralphie visits Father Intintola and even Rosalie comes to offer him support. He profusely apologizes to Rosalie for what had happened to her son, and in his first steps towards redemption for being a horrible human being in general, sets up a scholarship fund at Rutgers University for $20,000 in Jackie Aprile, Jr.'s name.

Meanwhile, Pie-O-My is badly burned in a stable fire and has to be put down. Tony, who comes to see the damage, is traumatised when he views the injured horse and the pain the fire had delivered her. He goes to visit Ralph to give him the news. Ralph, however, is more concerned with Justin and the growing cost of his medical care, and offers to make Tony eggs. Tony becomes suspicious that Ralph had the fire set to claim the insurance money on the horse, which Ralph denies. He almost has Tony convinced but then mocks Tony's concern. Furious, Tony starts a fight and eventually tackles Ralphie, chokes him, and bludgeons him to death, shouting "she was an innocent creature."

Tony calls Christopher to help him dispose of the body and again, he is high, which Tony rebukes him for. Tony tells Chris that Ralphie was dead when he got there, but Chris doesn't really believe him. They discuss how to handle the murder and what to say to their associates. They remove Ralph's head, hands, and feet and then wait until dark to dispose of everything. They throw headless body from a cliff and bury the rest at a farm (owned by Mikey Palmice's hospitalized father) - using a stolen JCB backhoe because the ground is frozen.

Junior has a rough time leaving court through a crowd of reporters and falls down the steps when hit by a boom. He has a short hospital stay, and though Junior suffered less lasting damage to his body than to his dignity, Tony calls Junior's attorney, Melvoin, and suggests that they could use this to their advantage by having Junior feign dementia and avoid trial.

Hits

- Ralph Cifaretto: beaten/strangled to death by Tony Soprano in a lengthy, rage-filled fist fight. His body was dismembered with the help of Christopher Moltisanti.

Trivia

- Tony uses the phrase "whoever did this" when discussing how others will react to Ralphie's death with Christopher.

- The title may also be considered to refer to the stable fire and Tony's suspicions of Ralphie.

- At two points in the episode, lines from the Rolling Stones song Sympathy for the Devil are quoted verbatim in reference to Ralph:

- When meeting with Justin's surgeon in the hospital, Ralph says, "Please allow me to introduce myself"

- When meeting with Father Phil, Ralph introduces himself with, "Pleased to meet you," ; shortly thereafter, Father Phil asks Ralph, "Were you there when Jesus Christ had his moment of doubt and pain?"

- Apollo 440's take on "The Man With The Harmonica" plays over the end credits.

"The Strong, Silent Type"

"The Strong, Silent Type" is the 49th episode of the HBO original series, The Sopranos. It was the 10th episode for the show's fourth season. The episode's teleplay was written by Terence Winter and Robin Green & Mitchell Burgess with a story by David Chase and was directed by Alan Taylor. It originally aired on Sunday November 17, 2002.

Guest Starring

- Tom Aldredge as Hugh De Angelis
- Sharon Angela as Rosalie Aprile
- Leslie Bega as Valentina La Paz
- Carl Capotorto as Little Paulie Germani
- Max Casella as Benny Fazio
- Dane Curley as Justin Cifaretto
- Joseph R. Gannascoli as Vito Spatafore
- Dan Grimaldi as Patsy Parisi
- Alla Kliouka Schaffer as Svetlana Kirilenko
- Elias Koteas as Dominic Palladino
- Marianne Leone as Joanne Moltisanti
- Richard Maldone as Ally Boy Barese
- Marissa Matrone as Ronnie Capozza
- Arthur J. Nascarella as Carlo Gervasi
- Suzanne Shepherd as Mary De Angelis

- Maureen Van Zandt as Gabriella Dante
- Karen Young as Agent Sanseverino

Synopsis

At a dinner with Silvio and Patsy, Albert verbalizes what many seem to be thinking: Tony killed Ralphie because of a mere racehorse. After Silvio leaves the table, Albert articulates his feeling that any boss who kills a member of his crew should be killed, and that if Tony had indeed killed Ralphie because of a horse, he would be the first in line to hit him.

When Furio returns from Italy, he has gifts for AJ and Meadow but nothing for Carmela. When she tells Rosalie about her feelings, Rosalie advises her not to consummate her relationship with Furio if she hasn't already.

Carmela receives a visit from Adriana, who bears quite a few bruises, and Adriana tells her that Christopher's enthusiasm for heroin has left him unstable. Junior compares Christopher to a beloved dog who gets rabies, saying he needs to be put out of his misery, but Tony disagrees, feeling his nephew is not an aging pet that needs to be put down. Instead, they organise an intervention. When Christopher wakes up one morning, his apartment is filled with friends and family and an intevention counselor. They all tell Christopher how his drug use has affected their lives, but Christopher frequently interrupts and insults them. When Paulie tells him to get his act together, Christopher starts making veiled references to their Pine Barrens debacle, which enrages Paulie, but confuses the intervention counselor. Tony becomes visibly upset when Adrianna reveals that Christopher, in addition to suffering from heroin-induced erectile dysfunction, accidentally killed her dog Cosette by sitting on her while high. Finally, when he calls his own mother a "whore", the intervention descends in to chaos. Christopher takes a beating from Silvio and Paulie and Christopher is taken to the emergency room with a hairline skull fracture.

At the hospital, Tony tells his nephew that the only reason he is alive is because, "you're my nephew and I love you." He arranges for Christopher to go to rehab and demands that he not leave until he is clean and sober, telling him that Patsy will be watching him.

Trivia

- The episode's title is a characteristic of Gary Cooper, which Tony often mentions in therapy. Tony first described Cooper this way in the "Pilot".

"Calling all Cars"

"Calling All Cars" is the 50th episode of the HBO original series, The Sopranos. It was the 11th episode in the show's fourth season. The episode was written by Robin Green & Mitchell Burgess, David Chase and David Flebotte and was directed by Tim Van Patten. It originally aired on Sunday November 24, 2002.

Guest Starring

- Ray Abruzzo as Little Carmine Lupertazzi
- Peter Bogdanovich as Dr. Elliot Kupferberg
- Richard Portnow as Attorney Melvoin
- Robert Funaro as Eugene Pontecorvo
- Tony Lip as Carmine Lupertazzi
- Paul Herman as Beansie Gaeta
- Joseph R. Gannascoli as Vito Spatafore
- Jessica Dunphy as Devin Pillsbury
- Angelo Massagli as Bobby Baccalieri, Jr.
- Lexie Sperduto as Sophia Baccalieri
- Alla Kliouka as Svetlana Kirilenko
- Elena Solovey as Branca Libinsk
- Tom Aldredge as Hugh DeAngelis
- Suzanne Shepherd as Mary DeAngelis
- Joe Marrizo as Joe Peeps

- Kevin Interdonato as Dogsy
- George Spaventa as V.I. Trifunovitch
- Steve Santosusso as Anthony
- Tony Darrow as Larry Barese
- Randy Barbee as Judge Whitney R. Runions
- Dan Castleman as Prosecutor
- Joe Pucillo as Beppy Scerbo
- Annabella Sciorra as Gloria Trillo

Synopsis

Tony has a dream where he rides in the back of his father's old cadillac, Carmela drives and Ralphie sits in front of him with a caterpillar on his bald head that changes into a butterfly. At first, Tony shares the back seat with Gloria Trillo, but then she morphs into Svetlana Kirilenko. Dr. Melfi suggests that it means that Carmela is in control and Tony wants to make peace with the ways in which he's impacted the lives of the other passenges of the car. Tony also expresses a dissatisfaction with his therapy and his lack of impulse control as it still leads him to make mistakes in his work. He makes reference to the fact that the money he spent on therapy could have gone towards a car and at least he would have got a blowjob out of that.

Bobby drops his daughter off at a baseball game and then takes a cake to Karen's grave and buries it. Later at dinner Bobby has to excuse himself from the table and go upstairs because he is upset. Janice questions Bobby and he initially lies but then tells her what he did with the cake as it would have been Karen and Bobby's 14 year anniversary. In Bobby Jr.'s room the children talk about ghosts and both are afraid. Janice visits Carmela at the Soprano household to talk to her about the difficulties Bobby is having in moving on.

Tony has a sitdown in New York with Carmine Lupertazzi and Johnny Sack. They demand 40% of his HUD business, as it is linked to Zellman. Tony refuses and splits, phoning Johnny on his way home with a counter of 5.5%, which Carmine refuses to talk about. Instead Carmine dispatches Joe Peeps to beat up Tony's appraiser on the HUD scam. He takes Anthony, an associate, with him and finds Vic the appraiser the next day.

Later Johnny meets with Paulie Walnuts and suggests that maybe they need to change leaders. Paulie is quick to put himself forward - reminding Johnny of his good relationship with New York. Johnny assures him that Carmine will always keep him in mind.

When Tony visits Junior at home to discuss getting to a juror in the RICO trial, Junior seems distracted and has a dishevelled appearance. Branca and Junior are not getting along very well. Later Tony has a meeting with Silvio Dante, Vito Spatafore and Paulie to discuss the disappearance of the appraiser. Eugene Pontecorvo arrives to pick up Vito and Paulie also reluctantly leaves. Once he is alone with Sil, Tony raises the possibility of reaching out to Little Carmine Lupertazzi in Florida through their old friend Beansie Gaeta. Vic gets beaten up again later -

this time by Vito and Dogsy from the Soprano family.

After Soprano Sunday dinner with the De Angelises and Baccalieri's, Anthony tries to disappear to his room with his girlfriend Devin. Carmela insists that he play a game with Bobby, Jr. and Sophia - AJ gets out the Ouija board and this progresses into a mock seance that scares the Baccalieri children. Tony gets a call from Beansie to confirm the trip, and Tony later and tells Silvio he suspects Paulie of being the leak through which Johnny is getting information on their business. He asks Silvio to keep the trip quiet from Paulie.

Svetlana calls Tony to thank him for sending her one of his horseshoe brooches. Tony seems very interested in continuing the relationship but Svetlana turns him down. In therapy Tony tells Dr. Melfi that he has broken Svetlanas heart but eventually admits that it was actually the other way around. He then concludes that he hasn't made much progress in therapy because he is high maintenance, and tells Dr. Melfi that he wants to leave therapy. Dr. Melfi counters that now that his symptoms are under control they can make real progress but Tony decides that her time is up, the fat lady has sung, and kisses Dr. Melfi on the cheek before he leaves.

At Junior's trial the judge throws out Melvoin's motion for a mistrial because government psychiatrists have seen through Junior's faux dementia act. Bobby, still optimistic, reassures Junior that they will get to a juror.

Bobby and Janice get into a fight at the mall over Bobby's continuing reluctance to let go of his wife. Later, Janice encourages the children via an internet chat client to use a Ouija board, and when Bobby arrives home his children have worked themselves into a state of near hysteria and he calls Janice for help. She tells him she had heard them with the ouija board earlier in the day but didn't want to get involved because she and Bobby were arguing. Janice uses her manufactured situation with the children as a reason that Bobby needs to move on and again asks him to eat Karen's ziti. Bobby agrees with a tear running down his face.

Tony arrives in Miami and meets up with Beansie. Later they meet with Little Carmine at a restaurant, who agrees to talk. Carmine seems eager to place the blame for the situation at Johnny's feet. Tony mentions that Carmine has tried to reach his Moulinade as well as beating up the appraiser.

Later, Tony has another dream where, is dressed in trousers, suspenders and a vest, he follows Ralph to an old house. He knocks on the door and a female figure descends slowly in shadow. The door creaks and Tony says he is there for the masoner job but does not speak English well. Just as Tony is about to enter the house he wakes up short of breath. He is still in Miami and is in a hotel.

First Appearances

- Carmine "Little Carmine" Lupertazzi: capo in the lupertazzi family and son of the boss, Carmine Sr.

Trivia

- Dr. Melfi uses the phrase "Calling All Cars" to signify her need for help when trying to reach Dr. Kupferberg after Tony quits therapy.

- The song "Surfing USA" by The Beach Boys plays over the closing credits

- The episode is the first to feature Tony's father's Cadillac.

- Ralphie reappears in this episode in Tony's dreams. Pantoliano is still credited in the opening sequence.

- Though credited, Jamie Lynn DiScala, Michael Imperioli, Drea de Matteo, Katherine Narducci and John Ventimiglia do not appear in this episode.

- It is revealed that Bobby Jr's AOL screen name is PowerBob386. After the airing of the episode, a real PowerBob386 AOL account was made and later sold on eBay

- In his dream Tony says he is at the house for a masoner job - his grandfather was a stonemason.

- Annabella Sciorra was credited for her appearance in Tony's dream.

- Peter Bogdanovich is credited in this episode, though only his voice on his answering machine is heard.

"Eloise"

"Eloise" is the 51st episode of the HBO original series, The Sopranos. It was the 12th episode for the show's fourth season. The episode was written by Terence Winter and was directed by James Hayman. It originally aired on Sunday December 1, 2002.

Guest Starring

- Ray Abruzzo as Little Carmine Lupertazzi
- Richard Portnow as Attorney Melvoin
- Matthew Del Negro as Brian Cammarata
- Robert Funaro as Eugene Pontecorvo
- Carl Capotorto as Little Paulie Germani
- Aleksa Palladino as Allesandra
- Sharon Angela as Rosalie Aprile
- Bruce MacVittie as Danny Scalercio
- Joseph R. Gannascoli as Vito Spatafore
- Tony Lip as Carmine Lupertazzi
- Dan Grimaldi as Patsy Parisi
- Fran Anthony as Minn Matrone
- France Esemplare as Nucci Gaultieri
- Anna Berger as Cookie Cirillo
- Max Casella as Benny Fazio
- Will Janowitz as Finn DeTrollio
- Evan Neuman as Colin McDermott

- Elaine Bromka as Ellen McDermott
- Jerry Grayson as Marty Schwartz
- Mark Lotito as Dave Fusco
- Kevin Interdonato as Dogsy
- Michael Goduti as Alfie
- Jeffrey M. Marchetti as Petey
- Brian McCormack as Greg Erwitt
- Dan Castleman as Prosecutor
- Joe Pucillo as Beppy Scerbo
- Gay Thomas-Wilson as Nurse

Synopsis

Junior's trial continues and Prosecutor Castleman makes his closing statement, referring the jury to the evidence gathered by the FBI agent that posed as a nurse at Dr Schreck's office. Junior gives the agent who posed as a nurse the stinkeye while Bobby looks carefully at the jurors to select the best candidate for intimidation.

At the Soprano household Carmela and AJ discuss a paper he is writing on Billy Budd and he learns that he has missed the homosexual subtext. Furio arrives and discusses his problems with the dampness in the new house with Carmela - she suggests her father may be able to help. Furio compliments Carmela's baking, and almost immediately afterwards, Tony comes downstairs and grabs a bite without any compliments or words of thanks. He tells Carm he has booked them a trip and is surprised when she is unreceptive. He makes the mistake of theorising that she got her hair cut because of their marital challenges. As Furio drives him he complains about Carmela, and Furio has difficulty restraining himself.

Little Carmine and Johnny Sack meet on the golf course and wait for Carmine, Sr. Little Carmine, despite initial dismissiveness and derisiveness by his father, describes his meeting with Tony. Johnny and Little Carmine try to tell Carmine he needs to come down from 40% but Carmine insults his son again by saying he would have been proud to have Tony as his own son. This prompts Little Carmine to tell his father that Tony has been complaining about the dispute over the appraiser. Little Carmine says that part of the problem may be Johnny and Tony's friendship, which Carmine doesn't seem overjoyed to hear.

Carmela visits Furio's house to discuss decorating. As Furio begins to tell her how special he thinks she is, they are interrupted by one of her father's contractors. They arrange to go looking for tiles together for the house.

Tony, Furio, Silvio, Patsy and Brian Cammarata are being entertained by Marty Schwartz at Chief Smith's casino and Furio refuses the offer of a trip upstairs with one of the girls. Brian, meanwhile, has had so much to drink that he is barely coherent, and they are ready to leave but have to wait for the limo. One of the girls suggests the helicopter. Marty calls Chief Smith and he allows them to use it to get home. Up on the landing platform they are greeted by their pilot Greg Erwitt. Tony and Furio stand near the tail rotor and Furio grabs hold of Tony as if to push him into their path, but when Tony asks Furio what he is doing he tells Tony he was standing too close to the blades.

Carmela visits Meadow's new apartment and meets her roommate Colin McDermott, and his mother Ellen. Ellen is full of praise for Meadow. Later, Meadow tells Carmela she is disappointed that her new boyfriend Finn hasn't yet told her he loves her.

The next day, Tony asks after Furio, who is late and tells Carmela he's going back to bed because of his hangover. As soon as Tony is upstairs and out of earshot, she calls Furio to check on him, but gets his machine. Soon thereafter, Meadow calls to invite her parents to eat at her new apartment on Sunday, and she is happy to report that Finn has invited her on a Canadian skiing trip. Carmela hears that Furio has put his house on the market. Carmela drives there immediately, but the place is completely empty.

Tony and Silvio attend a meeting with Johnny Sack at Carmine's new restaurant, and Tony is annoyed at Carmine's absence. Johnny offers 40% only on future deals instead of on all HUD deals. Tony and Silvio, unenthused about the offer, leave. Later that day, Carmela, Tony and AJ arrive in New York to have dinner with Meadow, and Tony gets a call from Silvio saying that Furio left a message at the Bing. Tony relays the news to Carmela that Furio has returned to Naples.

At Meadow's apartment, Finn introduces himself to Carmela and Tony. Tony is a big hit with Meadow's friends, making jokes and praising the food. Finn discusses AJ's college plans - he expects to go to Rutgers University. Carmela, however, becomes more miserable throughout the dinner and gets into an argument over the homosexual subtext of Billy Budd.

Little Paulie takes Petey and Alfie to vandalise Carmine's new restaurant, and later, Carmine is shown picking through the damages. At the Bing, Paulie complains to Silvio that Tony used his nephew for the job and he feels he is being kept in the dark. Silvio tells him his his payments have fallen behind those of the other capos. Paulie tells Silvio he is not worried however, because of his friendship with Tony, blaming Silvio for his problems saying that it all started when he had to make his collections and ended up in the Pine Barrens. Paulie calls Sil a "wormy cocksucker" but leaves before they descend into physical violence. Johnny visits Carmine and he gives an order to shut down work at the Esplanade. Later Vito, Patsy and Benny are shocked by the arrival of union reps at the construction site who close down work. Dave Fusco, the union representative, tells them the reason - employing non-union workers.

Eugene Pontecorvo and Dogsy catch up with juror Danny Scalercio while he is out shopping with his son. Gene comes up to him and talks to him about his family and tells him they know he will do the right thing. Vito meets with Sil and Tony to discuss the problems with construction. Tony decides to sit tight and wait for Carmine to cave as they will both lose money with construction shut down.

Carmela and Rosalie Aprile have dinner at Nuovo Vesuvio and Carmela confides in her that she misses Furio . When Ro suggests Tony may have realised and said something to Furio Carmela gets so upset she has to run to the bathroom. In NY Paulie is eating with Nucci, Minn and Cookie, and Cookie makes the mistake of practically announcing that Minn keeps her cash at home. Later, Carmela cries at home alone, interrupted by a phone call from Meadow who wants to meet for lunch at the Plaza. When she arrives for lunch Carmela is belligerent and picks a fight with Meadow but even though Carmela apologises, Meadow tells her she might transfer to Northwestern University to be closer to Finn.

Later at home, Tony asks Carmela about lunch at the plaza - she tells him it was horrible and she would be fine with never seeing Meadow again. Tony is shocked and they get in a fight, and then he stomps off, telling her he has enough on his plate already. While packing for her ski trip Meadow asks AJ about their mom's mood and he theorises that she is upset over Furio leaving. Tony asks Meadow to cut Carmela some slack and reveals that he and Carmela went to therapy together - Meadow didn't even know Tony was in therapy. He also suggests that Carm may be going through menopause - rather than tell her father what she had learned about Furio, Meadow agrees that it could be that.

Paulie attends a wedding where he "just happens" to bump into

Carmine. He tries to discuss the dispute between the two families, but when Carmine doesn't even recognise him, Paulie realises his shift in loyalties may have been premature. Later, Paulie breaks into Minn's house and starts to look for her cash and is caught. He tries to make excuses but Minn won't buy what he's trying to sell her; she knows his past and believes he is there to rob her. Paulie initially tries to calm her down, but when she cries for help and knees him in the crotch, he pounces on her and suffocates her with a pillow. He gets the money, and delivers a large envelope of cash to Tony. When Johnny calls, Paulie is quick to call him a prick, but Tony still sends him from the room. Anxious, Paulie listens from behind the door.

Tony drives to a clandestine meeting with Johnny, and Johnny tells Tony he wishes for Carmine's own sake that he would see sense on the Esplanade project. Tony questions John's motives in discussing this with him and Johnny surmises that the dispute would be over if something happened to Carmine. Tony is shocked, saying "holy shit" to himself after Johnny leaves. When he gets home, Carmela will barely speak to him about Meadow and asks if she has a fever. Carm reveals that she believes Meadow hates her, and is unresponsive when Tony tries to get her to take pleasure in their daughter's successes.

Hits

- Minn Matrone: suffocated by Paulie Walnuts after he attempted to steal her money and she saw him.

Trivia

- The title refers to the portrait "Eloise" at the Plaza Hotel which are based on the books of the same name.

"Whitecaps"

"Whitecaps" is the 52nd episode of the HBO original series, The Sopranos. It was the thirteenth and final episode of the show's fourth season. The episode was written by David Chase and Robin Green & Mitchell Burgess and was directed by John Patterson. It originally aired on Sunday December 8, 2002.

Guest Starring

- Bruce Altman as Alan Sapinsly
- Richard Portnow as Attorney Melvoin
- Carl Capotorto as Little Paulie Germani
- Liz Larsen as Trish Reingold-Sapinsly
- Cynthia Darlow as Virginia Lupo
- Bruce MacVittie as Danny Scalercio
- Dan Grimaldi as Patsy Parisi
- Tony Lip as Carmine Lupertazzi
- Max Casella as Benny Fazio
- Karen Young as Agent Robyn Sanseverino
- Alla Kliouka as Svetlana Kirilenko
- Okasana Lada as Irina Peltsin
- Tom Aldredge as Hugh DeAngelis
- Denise Borino as Ginny Sack
- Curtiss Cook as Credenzo Curtiss
- Universal as Stanley Johnson

- Matt Servitto as Agent Dwight Harris
- Frank Pando as Agent Frank Grasso
- Tony Darrow as Larry Barese
- Randy Barbee as Judge Whitney R. Runions
- Dan Castleman as Prosecutor
- Robert LuPone as Dr. Bruce Cusamano
- Will Janowitz as Finn Detrolio
- Joe Pucillo as Beppy Scerbo
- Jeffrey M. Marchetti as Petey

Synopsis

Tony gets a call from Patsy who is watching Adriana take Chris out of rehab, unawares that Agents Harris and Grasso are also watching. Dr. Cusamano, whose wife is still feeling porrly, reassures Carmela that it's probably mono Later, Tony takes Carmela to visit the house he is thinking of buying for the family on the Jersey shore. Carmela is concerned that it will be beyond their reach, but Tony explains that he wants something bring them together as a family. The realtor explains that there is a catch-the house has been sold to another couple but it seems likely that it will fall out of escrow. Later she encourages him to buy it as an investment but he cautions her about the follies of buying property for investment purposes.

Johnny is also worried over money with the esplanade shut down, and the stress causes strife between him and his wife Ginny. At Junior's trial the jury are having difficulty reaching a verdict and the jurors look angrily at one man in particular - Danny Scalercio - the juror Eugene Pontecorvo intimidated.

Chris drives Tony to meet Johnny and they discuss his rehabilitation from heroin addiction. The meeting takes place in an office max store and they again discuss making a move against Carmine. Tony says he has to pass, but when Johnny promises to relinquish claims to his HUD business and gives him an equitable split on future projects, Tony agrees to go ahead. On the return trip Tony discusses the job with Chris, and he asks Chris to contract the job out and make it look like a carjacking.

Tony and Chris visit whitecaps and Tony meets the owner, Alan Sapinsly. When Tony offers cash Sapinsly phones Dr. Kim, the current buyer, and negotiates his way out of their purchase agreement. Tony immediately tells his family the good news and they all arrive to look at the property. Meanwhile, Chris delivers a pre-payment to Credenzo Curtiss and John Clayborn - a couple of heroin dealers- and tells them about where they can catch Carmine.

Later, Irina phones the Soprano residence and gets AJ. She asks to speak to Carmela and tells her she used to fuck her husband, and distraught, Carmela hangs up on her. Irina calls back and tells Carmela that Tony loves her, and she also reveals his encounter with Svetlana. Carmela tells Irina if she calls again then she will find her and kill her, then going into a frenzy and putting Tony's stuff out on the lawn. Tony pulls into his drive and runs over his golf clubs, witnessing Carmela throwing more of his stuff from the window as he gets out of the car. She throws things at him when he enters the house and locks herself in the bedroom, screaming that he has embarrassed her for years with his infidelity and is angry because it has seeped into their home lives. Tony tries to deny everything and when Carmela draws her hand back to slap him, Tony restrains her and throws her against the wall. She retreats to the bedroom and tells him to leave the house, again becoming violent when he touches her. Tony accuses Carmela of taking money from his stash in the bird feed. Carmela counters by bringing up the fingernail she found - Tony tries to deny the connection but stumbles when he realizes he was about to say it belonged to someone else. Carmela again insists Tony leave, when Tony asks about the kids she admits it is horrible for them but stands her ground.

Tony drives to Irina's duplex but only Svetlana is there. Svetlana tells Tony that Irina and Zellman broke up because of his beating, and tells Tony that Branca was the one who told Irina about their affair. Tony goes to whitecaps to sleep. In the morning he is awoken by Sapinsly banging on the window, asking him not to stay in the house. After getting dressed, Tony asks to withdraw from the sale but Alan insists that they adhere to the contract. Trish chastises Alan for getting into a dispute with a mob boss after Tony leaves and also for lying about having partners.

Adriana meets with Agent Sanseverino and they discuss Chris' return. Adriana says that Chris feels he is unfit to be a father after killing her dog, and tells Robyn that she and Chris plan to get Ralphie help when he resurfaces. She also tells them that Vito has been calling her while Chris was in rehab. Finally she asks permission to visit her mother, and they consent.

Tony gets a call from Johnny to tell him Carmine has decided to settle. Tony and Chris attend a sitdown in Queens and they settle on 15% for Carmine. Johnny, however, is visibly put out. Carmine asks Tony to remember Little Carmine's role in the settlement after he is gone but reminds them of his good health.

At the Soprano household, Meadow discusses the separation with her mother. She is distraught about it and brings up Furio, but Carmela denies any infidelity and Meadow storms off after asking her mother how she could eat shit from Tony for so many years. Tony eats at Nuovo Vesuvio and Artie offers consolations - Tony's response is to criticize the food. Johnny rings Tony to ask if the hit is still on, and Tony confirms that it is still scheduled as a go.

At the Bing, Paulie talks to Silvio about Johnny Sack and suggests Ralphie may have been in cahoots with him. Chris and Tony arrive, and Paulie tells Tony he would put Carmela out on the street if she were his wife. Patsy says that he couldn't disrupt the kids like that. Sapinsly phones Tony to say he is going to let him out of the sale but will keep the deposit. Tony respondes that if that's the case he will move in and make their lives hell.

Tony returns home and Carmela, shocked to see him, tries to stop him taking food from the fridge and threatens a restraining order. Tony gets violent and refuses to leave, and Carmela runs upstairs. Later AJ helps Tony clear the home cinema room so that he can stay there.

Chris exercises at home and Adriana drinks wine even though he yells at her for drinking around him. Tony calls Chris to call off the hit, telling him he must make sure that the hired guns don't talk to anyone. Later, Chris meets Credenzo and Clayborn with the rest of their payment and drives off, and then Benny and Petey shoot the two would-be hitmen before they can drive away.

Back at the Soprano house Tony lies in the pool and Carm asks him to move the chairs he has put on the lawn, which sets off another argument. Carm tells Tony it might not have come to this if he had a more loving attitude while at home. Tony asks her what she expected from their marriageas she knew everything about him when they met, accusing her of being materialistic and attracted to his power. Carmela calls Tony hateful and reveals her feelings for Furio, telling Tony that her happiest moments for months have been her mornings with Furio: when Tony came downstairs, she felt like someone who had a terminal illness but had forgotten about it for a while. Tony tells her he looked for women with different qualities from her in his affairs, but she reminds him that he hardly knew most of the women he slept with and walks out, calling him a hypocrite. Tony later calls Dr. Melfi but hangs up when she answers.

Junior finally gets his mistrial when the jury still cannot reach a verdict because of intimidated juror Danny Scalercio. When

Junior gets home he is not in the mood for a celebration and just lets Bobby order pizza.

AJ goes to his father to ask if he can move in with him because he is not getting along with his mother. Tony realizes his presence at the house is damaging for his children. Tony ends his talk with AJ by giving him money to buy his mother a gift and tell her he is sorry. Benny and Little Paulie take the speakers out on the Stugots and play a Dean Martin concert at high volume, disrupting the Sapinsly's luncheon.

Tony drives out to meet Johnny and tell him that the Carmine hit is off. His thinking is that the hit will be to high profile and that there is no reason to kill Carmine now that the dispute is resolved. John is enraged and complains to Tony that he will have to go back to work for Carmine and his son, who he hates - Tony says he shouldn't be hearing this. Tony returns home and tells the family he has decided to move out. AJ becomes upset and asks if it was because he asked to live with Tony. Meadow takes the news hard as well and suggests Tony go back to therapy, later going upstairs to cry.

Tony packs to leave and Carmela asks him to be careful, standing in the doorway with her son and watching him drive away. Back at the Sapinsly house the harassment continues - as soon as they venture outside the music begins again. After realizing that this could continue indefinitely, they agree to give Tony his money back.

Hits

- Stanley Johnson: shot by Benny Fazio and Petey in the Meadowlands to ensure his silence about the cancelled Carmine hit.
- Credenzo Curtiss: shot by Benny Fazio and Petey in the Meadowlands to ensure his silence about the cancelled Carmine hit.

Trivia

- James Gandolfini won his third Emmy Award for his performance in this episode.

- Edie Falco won her third Emmy Award for her performance in this episode.

- John Patterson won Outstanding Directorial Achievement in Dramatic Series from the Directors Guild of America for his work on this episode.

- Robin Green, Mitchell Burgess and David Chase won the Emmy in Outstanding Writing for a Drama Series for their work on this episode.

- David Chase described Tony's use of Dean Martin to intimidate Sapinsly as cultural warfare because Martin is Italian.

- Adriana describes Vito as Ralph's second in command.

- The episode ran for 75 minutes -- currently the longest Sopranos episode to date.

Index

Agent Sanseverino ... 103, 126, 150
Asbury Park 58
Bada Bing . 39, 40, 41, 82, 108, 114
Barone Sanitation .. 13, 41
birthday 39, 54, 57, 90
cancer . 33, 34, 35, 36, 44, 67, 74
Columbia University ... 12, 24, 39
Crazy Horse 55, 69, 92, 93
cumare 63
David Chase . 2, 11, 15, 18, 19, 30, 38, 66, 72, 80, 89, 113, 125, 129, 146, 154
DiMeo 13, 85
Directors Guild of America 154
Dr. Melfi ... 23, 28, 30, 32, 41, 45, 50, 51, 52, 54, 64, 67, 75, 85, 90, 108, 110, 119, 130, 132, 135, 152
dream 29, 44, 61, 109, 130, 133, 136
drug 55, 73, 82, 126
Edgar Allan Poe 56
Emmy 30, 153, 154
Emmy award 30
FBI . 12, 13, 16, 33, 44, 59, 60, 61, 74, 81, 82, 83, 92, 114, 115, 139
funeral . 17, 33, 75, 76, 119

gambling 75
Globe Motors .. 50, 51, 52, 67
Green Grove 118
heroin 82, 84, 126, 148
jury 139, 148, 152
New Jersey 17, 28, 55
New York ... 24, 45, 65, 76, 81, 100, 131, 141
Northwestern University 143
Nuovo Vesuvio 22, 29, 60, 108, 110, 143, 150
Outstanding Directorial Achievement 153
panic attack 23, 75
Point Pleasant 28
priest 67
RICO trial 19, 74, 131
Russian mob ... 30, 59, 62
Rutgers University 23, 60, 122, 142
St. Peter 22
Svetlana. 15, 16, 17, 18, 21, 30, 59, 121, 125, 129, 130, 132, 146, 149
Thanksgiving 50
The Matrix 54, 57
The Public Enemy 18
therapy 28, 30, 41, 52, 54, 75, 85, 108, 110, 127, 130, 132, 135, 143, 152
wire 17, 45, 59
Writers Guild of America 65

www.ingramcontent.com/pod-product-compliance
Lightning Source LLC
Chambersburg PA
CBHW032300150426
43195CB00008BA/519